THE SILENT HEROES

VOLUME I

FEB. 22, 1944 – JULY 21, 1944

Manuel F. van Eyck

Copyright 1990 by Manuel F. van Eyck

TURNER PUBLISHING COMPANY

TURNER PUBLISHING COMPANY

Turner Publishing Company Staff:
Editor: Amy Sietsma
Designer: Peter Zuniga

Library of Congress Control No.
2002104277

ISBN: 978-1-68162-172-2

Additional copies may be purchased directly from the
publisher. Limited Edition.

ABBREVIATIONS

BG   Bomb Group

BS   Bomb Squadron

FG   Fighter Group

FS   Fighter Squardron

TO THE MEMORY OF THE FALLEN AMERICAN AIRMEN WHO PARTICIPATED IN AIR OPERATIONS OVER OCCUPIED CZECHOSLOVAKIA 1944-1945

DEDICATED TO MY PARENTS

Back row, l-r: lst Lt. G.M. Goddard Jr., 2nd Lt. H. Kandarian, 2nd Lt. C.F. Spickard, 2nd Lt. J.F. Altemus. Front Row, L-R: T/Sgt. R.A. Noury, S/Sgt. W.E. Nelson, S/Sgt. H.C. Carter, S/Sgt. Adams*, S/Sgt. R.E. Hughes. *S/Sgt. Adams not on mission to Regensburg.

ACKNOWLEDGMENTS

The Silent Heroes is the culmination of over 10 years research. Needless to say, it would not have been possible without the support of many official agencies, former airmen of 8th, 9th and 15th AF and many people in USA, France, Belgium, Italy, England and Czechoslovakia.

At National Archives they were:

Amy Schmidt
Richard L. Boylan
Dewilda M. Williams
Rebecca A. Lentz
Elaine C. Everly
Wilna Uebrick-Pacheli

At Department of the Air Force they were:

Maj. Lester A. Sliter
Lt. Col. Jacobson
2nd Lt. Johnson
Harry Fletcher
Frederick J. Shaw Jr.
Capt. George Cully
Dr. Haulman
Lynn O. Gamma
Dr. James H. Kitchens
Bruce Ashcroft
Archie DiFante
Dr. Robert M. Johnson II
MSgt. Bailey
Cargill Hall
Dr. Timothy A. Warnock
Col. John Schenk
Maj. Branum
Nora Bledsoe
Carolyn Mandler
2nd Lt. Kyle R. Richard.

At Department of the Army there was John F. Manning and Thomas L. Sherlock.

At Veteran Administration they were:

Dennis E. Kuehl
Steve L. Muro
Jimmy S. Adamson
Robert St. Clair
Ralph E. Church
Gary D. Peak
Patricia K. Novak.

In Belgium they were Jacques R. Adelee and Bart Beckers.

In France they were Paul Bodot. In England there was Mrs. Follas.

In New Zealand there was Harry Widdup.

In Czechoslovakia they were:

Lubomir Caletka
Stefan Mikulcik
Peter Mazur
Bozena Pesatova
Dr. Milos Ruzicka
Josef Smejkal
Pavel Skodacek
Pavel Tresnak
Ruzena Pernikarova
Vladislav Kunes
Pavel Palecek
Antonin Kuchar
Bedrich Simanek
Otakar Vanecek

Ing. Jan Smejkal
Josef Lomoz
Vladimir Chocholousek
Ing. Ivan Hulka
Karel Stava
Jan Svamberg
Pavel Lachman
Peter Kames
Oldrich Hanka
Gerda Stulcova
Ervin Pospisil
Stanislav Mares
Roger Klima MD
Teodor Kujan
M. Kraftova
Zdenek Tafl
Josef Soucek
Magda Vodrazkova
J. Rychetsky
Frantisek Vesely
Ruzena Hosnova
Tomas Podlaha
Jan Sandera
Ing. Alois Vyhnalek
Jaroslav Raska.

In the USA the Police Departments that assisted me:

City/Town

Merrill, WI
Shelton, WA
Roxboro, NC
Davenport, IA
Maj. Ron Potter
Marshalltown, IA
Capt. Ronald L. Galloway
Union, OR
Chief William Hudson
Huntingdon, PA
Chief William J. Brkovich
North Richland Hills, TX
Chief Dr. J.L. McGlasson
Maquoketa, IA
Chief Ronald Evans
Findlay, OH
Chief David B. Clark
West Hartford, CT
Det. Sgt. Francis X. Gallagher
Chappell, NE
Hartford, CT
Chief Bernard R. Sullivan
Springfield, MO
Michael Batson
Jackson, MS
Sgt. M.L. Dill
Italy, TX
Chief R.W. Wilkinson
Scranton, PA
Daniel Ebersole
Twin City, MI
Sgt. Cindy M. Barrette
Needham, MA
Chief Louis Roman
Pulaski, TN
Chief Stanley E. Newton
Oostburg Fire Department, WI
Fire Chief Glen Bruggink

The following associations offered their help:

Louis Loevsky
466th BG
Floyd Mabee
2nd Air Div.
George Baroni
98th BG
Victor Meeker
450th BG
S/Sgt. R.H. Armstrong
455th BG
Norv Gage
456th BG
Thomas L. Thomas
96th BG
Pastor Eugene Parker
463rd BG
George R. Hilliard
398th BG
John Devney
459th BG
Jacob L. Grimm
483rd BG
Chester E. Konkolewski
485th BG
Bud Markel
461st BG
Edward J. Huntzinger
388th BG
Charles Konsler
4th FG
Jack T. Curtis
367th FG
Edwin Dalrymple
31st FG
Joseph DeShay
357th FG
Thomas S. Thomas III
464th BG
Tony Chardwlla
359th FG

My sincere thanks goes to these individual airmen:

Col. Jerome L. Loewenberg
Robert R. Kirsch
Robert A. Norvell
James T. Creekmore
LTC Albert J. Bischoff
Kenneth Faulk
Edgar A. Squires
Edward A. Kunssler
Charles A. Gahagan
Morris Goldberg
Donald E. Harder
Henry J. Kreiensieck
Rufus A. Ward
Robert P. Reynolds
Clifton J. Stewart
Francis W. Flynn
Bryce K. Johnson
Col. B.A. Strozier
Paul W. Pease
Cyril J. Carver
Richard Pemberton
Thomas Smith Jr.
R.W. Mazzacane
Andrew Kolenic
Paul E. Brenneman
LTC C.P. Huntington
R.C. Harris Jr.
Warren E.C. Wacker, M.D.

LTC Bill Haskins
Paul E. Sumner
LTC Stanley A. Hutchins
Charles G. Dreyer
BG John W. Baer
A.O. Tice
Wilbur R. Richardson
Thomas R. Monacelli
Marvin L. Jarchow
Thomas W. Qualman
Donald L. Gallagher
Irwin H. Glickman
BG O.T. Ridley
B.M. Morey
Walter F. Freeman
Dennis Brown
Walter R. Miller
William P. Brierty
G. Carney
R.H. Powell
Irving Welsted
Richard Wynn
Milton A. Klarsfeld
Col. R.D. Carlson
Wilfrid E. Hebert
Paul W. Capen
Louis Fliegelman
Katzenmeyer
John R. Johnson
William "Ike" Adamson
Raymond A. Noury
Ralph W. Kittle
Col. A.J. Diefendorf
Carl F. Runge
Hobart A. Jarvis
Charles W. Bratton
Lawrence M. Eidsmore
James Watson
Arnold Moselle

My sincere thanks goes to the relatives of men killed in action over occupied Czechoslovakia:

Gertrude Aylesworth
Karen Attanasio
R.L. and V.B. Cruthis
Rose Sebelski
H.J. "Doc" Weiler
Russel Reese
Ruth Young
Esco Vaughn
Marguerite E. Vralsted
Sidney J. Bowlin
Samuel B. Black, M.D.
E. Roberts
Norman E. Simay
E. Yesia
Ed N. Harrison
Roy L. Bumgardner
Marvin Jarchow
Jim Kingsnorth
Jesse McSwain
Edward Wiley
Mrs. Rundbaken
Marion J. Roberts
Henrieta Thomas
Thomas J. Clark
David Webster
Jimmy Sallings
Merl Q. Vanderhoof

22 FEB 1944, 15TH AF, 98TH BG, 343RD BS

Target: Regensburg, Germany
Aircraft type, model and series: B-24J, Serial No. 42-73138-U
Engines - type, model and series: R-1830-65
Engine Nos. (a) 42-88581, (b) 42-39205, (c) 42-33577, (d) 42-39079
Nickname of aircraft: Unknown
Type of mission: Bombing.
Aircraft last seen at 1230 hours at 48/00 N, 12/40 E. Aircraft was lost as result of enemy aircraft.
Point of departure: Fortunate Cesare A/D, Italy

CREW POSITION, NAME IN FULL:

Goddard, George M. Jr.	1st Lt, Pilot	0-725718	KIA
Kandarian, Haig	2nd Lt, Copilot	0-527673	KIA
Altemus, Joseph F.	2nd Lt, Nav.	0-732425	KIA
Spickard, Charles F.	2nd Lt, Bomb.	0-668813	KIA
Houser, Oscar W.	T/Sgt, Eng.	20315036	KIA
Noury, Raymond A.	T/Sgt, RO	11031403	POW
Rhodes, Rexford H.	S/Sgt, Asst. Eng.	17015953	KIA
Carter, Harold C.	S/Sgt, Gunner	36434112	KIA
Hughes, Roy E.	S/Sgt, Tail Gunner	38107151	KIA
Goldbach, John A.	S/Sgt, Nose Gunner	33188500	KIA
Nelson, Waynworth E.	S/Sgt, Asst. RO	16096103	KIA

1st Lt. George M. Goddard Jr. and 2nd Lt. Haig Kandarian

S/Sgt. Rexford H. Rhodes receiving DFC from Gen. Doolittle 30 Oct 1943

Out of the desert in a cafe and first meal in Tel Aviv: Sgt. Robert J. Judy, Sgt. Ernest E. Sestina, S/Sgt. Clement S. Badeau, S/Sgt. Francis S. Beatty, S/Sgt. Rexford H. Rhodes (who also participated in mission to Ploesti on 1 Aug 1943, Pilot Lt. Glen W. Underwood, B-24 "Northern Star")

S/Sgt. Rexford H. Rhodes with his crew after raid on Ploesti/

FAITHFUL TO THE END

PILOT 1ST LT. GEORGE M. GODDARD JR., 0-725718

A man with strength, steady nerves and courage, he knew his aircraft and handled them like it was his right arm. A straight guy and one who loved his work and his wife.

COPILOT 2ND LT. HAIG "KANDY" KANDARIAN, 0-527673

Tops with everything and everyone who knew him; a flying sergeant once; attended engineering, gunnery and armament school, graduating as EM. He was unlucky at love and cards, but a great guy.

NAVIGATOR 2ND LT. JOSEPH F. "ALTIMETER/ STAR GAZER" ALTEMUS, 0-732425

Happy go lucky, full of pep, eager and always getting us home on the minute. He was joking and full of fun anytime you met him.

BOMBARDIER 2ND LT. CHARLES F. SPICKARD, 0-668813

A guy who attained results, worked hard at his job and always hit the target with accuracy. He loved good times and was a swell egg.

ENGINEER T/SGT. OSCAR V. "LUCKY" HOUSER, 20315036

Was on Ploesti raids and had a tough time, but fought to the end, always at his best. A fellow to have around with strong mind and kind heart, he was good looking and loved to have a good time.

TOP TURRET S/SGT. ROY E. HUGHES, 38107151

The best gunner I ever knew. He was cool and quiet, talking was his best past time. He worked with efficiency and always a smile. He loved his family with all his heart and was one who never forgot a buddy.

BALL TURRET S/SGT. HAROLD C. CARTER, 36434112

An eager, attractive, pleasant and intelligent speaker, he had what it takes to get on top, always putting his heart and soul in everything he did. He loved best to write home and to his girl.

NOSE GUNNER S/SGT. REXFORD H. "DUSTY" RHODES, 17015953

Another Ploesti boy who had gone through the mills and believed to be his last mission. He was quiet and loved by everyone, a true friend and would give you his shirt if needed be. A guy worth fighting for, he was honest and brave.

TAIL GUNNER S/SGT. WAYNWORTH E. "LORD NELSON" NELSON, 16096103

One in a million, he was clean and well spoken, always cheerful, happy and full of confidence. Quiet, easy to get along with and very seldom went out. He never spoke a harsh word, his temper always normal. He was the best pal a fellow would ever want. I loved him best because I always wanted to be a good gunner like him.

22 FEB 1944, OUR LAST MISSION

I guess we all feel something strange or some little incidents whenever things are apt to go wrong. Well, that morning I felt it inside, of course, it was only after everything happened that they came to me. First it was Sgt. Adams who was taken sick at the last minute (had a lot of confidence and never flown without him), so T/Sgt. Oscar W. Houser replaced him. I noticed he was a little nervous, but knowing what happened the mission before (a close call when a big piece of flak knocked the flashlight out of his hands when trying to fix a generator) and it was also getting close to the end of his missions, so it was natural that he should be nervous.

After briefing at the Intelligence Office, usually 1st Lt. M. "George" Goddard Jr., 2nd Lt. Haig "Kandy" Kandarian, 2nd Lt. Charles F. "Spick" Spickard and 2nd Lt. Joseph F. "Joe" Altemus arrived at the aircraft together, but that morning Joe wasn't himself. The eagerness and happy-go-lucky smile were not there. I always liked to kid him about the target, but that morning I just couldn't say anything. About 10 minutes later Joe told us the target was Regensburg, the furthermost point ever hit in Germany by the 15th Air Force, and before we had a chance to say anything, George called us together and said, "Boys, it's Regensburg and you can expect the worst—no fighter escort, so keep your guns working and your eyes open at all times. Check it often and report if anything goes wrong. O.K. Check them before we take off." He felt a little nervous for the first time since I knew him. We were carrying 10 five hundred lb. bombs, made a swell take off at about 08.05 hours and the target to be reached at about 13.00 hours. Other groups were 10 minutes ahead of us—a total of 69 ships, the biggest number we ever went on a target with.

The second thing I noticed was when sitting at my radio position before we got in high altitude, we had taken our gun position facing "Dusty" S/Sgt. Rexford H. Rhodes, and he stared in the corner with a twinkle in his eyes and white as a sheet. I didn't dare say anything, realizing it was the last mission of his required 50 missions. The weather was fair, but we hit air pockets a couple of times. Once we got into a prop wash, but George handled the aircraft well. We had a lot of confidence in George; he had a name for himself, Kandy, and was always pleased to sit up and sweat it out.

It was about 40 or 45 below zero as we were crossing the Alps. Ship after ship was turning back—that we did not like because we knew we were losing firing power. When we got to the turning point, we again had to face Tail End Charlie, the last aircraft in the group and not protected by any of the other aircraft in the formation.

Then the flak started to come up and we were hit pretty bad. There were holes all over, but we kept flying. The weather didn't look too good. Just as the enemy fighters started to come up, I called S/Sgt. Waynworth E. Nelson to keep his eyes open because one of our aircraft (Lt. Siemen's Crew) was struggling behind and to try to help them out.

On the first attack the wing of Lt. Siemen's ship between number one and number two engine fell off, and being just in my view I watched it go down until it disappeared out of sight. I saw no one bail out, and later I met only one man, the ball turret gunner.

Then S/Sgt. Harold C. Carter, our ball turret gunner, called up saying his guns jammed. George answered "Do your best and get them working." About one half minute later, Carter said he had one working. Then I heard Spick call up and say "Bombs Away." Nelson was firing away and reloaded his guns. It was then that I smelled gas through my oxygen mask, so I took it and also my interphone off. I went to check the bomb bay and realized the danger—gas was flowing in the bomb bay. Having just dropped our bombs, I went back to the waist to help S/Sgt. John A. Golbach put his chute on, then went to the tail to tell Nelson. Flak was still hitting us, so when I returned to the waist, Golbach gave me a sign to check the ball turret as it had been hit. I tried to bring it up hydraulically but no success. I tried the door and it was jammed, so wanting to call George up, I returned to the waist to get on the interphone. As I looked out the left waist window, eight fighters, ME-110, were ready to attack. Seeing that "Goldy" was waiting too long to fire, I got a little anxious and hollered for him to shoot, "Let'em have it," and he waited until the fourth one peeled off. I noticed 20mm balls of fire heading for us. Realizing I was getting weak from lack of oxygen, I turned around to put my mask on and started to fire at a fighter, but my mask fell off as I started to check number three and number four engines—they were on fire. All of a sudden I noticed the wing peeling off and the aircraft was going into a dive on the right. I told myself it was the end and reached for my crucifix, but couldn't find it. I blacked out and finally woke up at about 3 or 4,000 feet. My chute was full of holes, the grip handle still in its place (it had opened by itself), no shoes and my microphone was still tied to me. I landed in about three feet of snow and didn't even see the aircraft go down or anything. I thought probably they had gone back and I was thrown out or dumped out in the dive. So that's the story. The only information I got was when I met Lt. Jones in Nurnberg, Germany. He was shot-down in April 1944. What he told me was that the intelligence officer in my squadron gave a report that the aircraft went into a dive, started to pull out of it and blew up. Two chutes were seen to open, but the other has never been accounted for.

This statement was prepared by the only survivor T/Sgt. Raymond A. Noury.

22 FEB 1944, 15TH AF, 98TH BG, 415TH BS

Target: Regensburg, Germany
Aircraft type, model and series: B-24D, Serial No. 42-40662
Engines - type, model and series: R-1830-43
Engine Nos: (a) 42-65657 (b) 42-37665 (c) 41-15041 (d) 42-87984
Nickname of aircraft: *Black Magic*
Type of mission: Bombing
Aircraft last seen at 1320 hours at 48/03 N, 13/10 E. Aircraft was lost as result of enemy aircraft.
Point of departure: Italy

CREW POSITION, NAME IN FULL:

Malas, Donald E.	1st Lt, Pilot	0-796417	POW
Brady, Edwin N.	2nd Lt, Copilot	0-802709	POW
Williams, Horace L.	1st Lt, Nav.	0-676809	POW
Hawley, Charles H.	1st Lt, Bomb.	0-676484	POW
Vanderhoof, Merl Q.	T/Sgt, Eng/Gunner	36061472	POW
Hart, Jesse C.	T/Sgt, ROG	18037589	POW
Brinkman, John G.	S/Sgt, Gunner	11100929	POW
Dabek, Wladyslaw C.	S/Sgt, Gunner	11113888	POW
Schwartz, Saul	S/Sgt, Gunner	32462688	POW
Tropeano, Ralph	S/Sgt, Gunner	32407033	POW

Front row, l-r: S/Sgt. John G. Brinkman, S/Sgt. Wladyslaw C. Dabek, S/Sgt. Ralph Tropeano, T/Sgt. J. Philips (not on this mission), T/Sgt. Jesse C. Hart Back row, l-r: T/Sgt. Merl Q. Vanderhoof, 1st Lt. Charles H. Hawley, 1st Lt. Horace L. Williams, 2nd Lt. Don Manger (not an this mission), lst Lt. Donald E. Malas (2nd Lt. Edwin N. Brady and S/Sgt. Saul Schwartz are not in this photo)

Over Brux (Most), Czechoslovakia

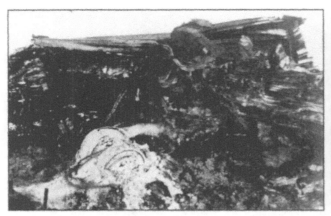

Wreckage of the "Black Magic" B-24D near Lhenice, Czechoslovakia

STATEMENT BY 2ND LT. EDWIN N. BRADY, 0-802709

Our aircraft left formation approximately 80 miles east of Regensburg, Germany. All of crew bailed out in an approximately the same location.

Exact location where our aircraft struck the ground is unknown. Heard ship strike.

1st Lt. D.E. Malas wounded on head; S/Sgt. J.G. Brinkman and S/Sgt. Dabek severely wounded in legs; 1st Lt. H.L. Williams sprained knee on landing; myself wounded slightly face, right shoulder, right leg.

Other crew members wounded slightly or none at all. Last saw Sgts. Hart, Vanderhoof, Schwartz, Tropeano at Frankfurt, Germany.

1st Lt. Malas, Lt. Williams, Lt. Hawley and myself at Stalag Luft I, Barth.

After liberation saw all of crew except S/Sgt. S. Schwartz at Camp Lucky Strike, France.

S/Sgt. Saul Schwartz, 32462688

S/Sgt. Schwartz bailed out approximately 80 miles east of Regensburg, Germany. Last contact when I removed him from top turret; oxygen line punctured, suffered temporary anoxia.

12 MAY 1944, 8TH AF, 357TH FG, 364TH FS

Target: Brux (Most), Czechoslovakia
Aircraft type, model and series: P-51B, Serial No. 42-106777
Engine - type, model and series: V-1650-7, Serial No. V-320315
Nickname of aircraft: Unknown
Type of mission: Ramrod
Place of departure: Station F-373
Aircraft last sighted at 1250 hours 10 miles northwest of Schweinfurt, Germany. Aircraft was lost as a result of enemy aircraft.

CREW POSITION, NAME IN FULL

Carder, John B.   Capt, Pilot   0-740364   POW

REPORT ON SHOT - DOWN AMERICAN AIRCRAFT

Date and time aircraft was shot-down: 12 May 1944 at 1300 hours.
Place of crash: 20 km of northwest of Giessen/2 km north of Bischoffen, Herbon, county of Biedenkopf
Kind of capture: belly landing
Type of aircraft: Mustang

Markings: C5*J, No. 2106777

The aircraft was shot upon and made a belly landing on a meadow. Wings and tail unit are badly damaged, the underside of the fuselage is torn open. The propeller is damaged.

Crew: Capt. John Carder, 740364

Place and time of capture: On 12 May 1944 about 1900 hours at Offenbach, Dillkreis, Germany

12 May 1944, 8th AF, 452nd BG, 728th BS

Target: Brux (Most), Czechoslovakia

Aircraft type, model and series: B-17G, Serial No. 42-107089

Engine - type, model and series: R-1820-97

Engines Nos. (a) SW-011141 (b) SW-010989 (c) SW-011123 (d) SW-011077

Nickname of aircraft: Unknown

Type of mission: Bombing. Aircraft was lost as a result of enemy aircraft. Last seen at 1220 hours approximately at 50/17 N, 07/40 E.

Point of departure: AAF STA 142

Crew position, name in full

Slanin, Boris	1st Lt, Pilot	0-728032	KIA
Tuttle, Robert M.	LtCol, Copilot	0-23745	POW
Mortin, Irving	F/O, Nav.	T-122846	POW
Prigmore, Charles S.	2nd Lt, Bomb	0-744023	POW
Goodwin, Russell M.	T/Sgt, TTG	34305942	POW
Griffin, Robert M.	T/Sgt, RO	38195073	POW
McRay, Eugene	S/Sgt, BTG	16073946	POW
Giombetti, Rinaldo V.	S/Sgt, LWG	31159788	POW
Palmeter, Clarence F.	S/Sgt, RWG	12031192	KIA
Myren, Fred L.	2nd Lt, TG	0-757647	KIA

Statement by Lt. Col. Robert M. Tuttle, 0-23745

Our aircraft left formation north of Frankfurt, Germany. Bombardier 2nd Lt. Charles S. Prigmore and Navigator F/O Irving Mortin bailed out of nose door; waist gunners, ball turret, top turret went out waist door; Copilot out tail door and pilot I don't know.

The pilot, lst Lt. Boris Slanin, was last seen after the order to bail out was given. At that time he was getting out of his seat and was uninjured.

1st Lt. Boris Slanin, 0-728032

1st Lt. Slanin was last seen getting out of his seat. At the time the cockpit was in flames. His chute may have burned, in such a case he may have tried to ride it in or jumped with a burning chute.

S/Sgt. Clarence F. Palmeter, 12031192

S/Sgt. Palmeter did not bail out. S/Sgt. Palmeter was struck in stomach and shoulders by 20mm shells and was left for dead in the radio room.

2nd Lt. Fred L. Myren, 0-757647

2nd Lt. Myren bailed out from the tail door. Last contact on interphone about 10 minutes before routine check. The pilot of a ship directly behind in the formation is said to have seen him bail out and strike the nose of his ship. This would place the time of his jump at about five minutes before the rest of the crew. 2nd Lt. Myren was the first to jump. At that time the ship had been only heavily damaged and still in formation.

12 MAY 1944, 8TH AF, 452ND BG, 728TH BS

Target: Brux (Most), Czechoslovakia
Aircraft type, model and series: B-17G, Serial No.: 42-97209
Engine - type, model and series: R-1820-97
Engines Nos. (a) SW-011756 (b) SW-011709 (c) SW-011439 (d) SW-011497
Nickname of aircraft: Unknown
Type of mission: Bombing. Aircraft was lost as a result of enemy aircraft. Last seen at 1220 hours approximately at 50/17 N, 07/40 E.
Point of departure: AAF STA 142

CREW POSITION, NAME IN FULL

Hochstetter, Herbert C.	2nd Lt, Pilot	0-754008	POW
Hurst, Julian M.	2nd Lt, Copilot	0-815146	POW
Brown, Clyde D.	2nd Lt, Nav.	0-700696	POW
Kogitz, Jerome	2nd Lt, Bomb.	0-757528	POW
Ventura, John J.	S/Sgt, TTG	31240869	POW
Jenkins, James T.	S/Sgt, RO	14103655	POW
Rase, Hans A.	S/Sgt, BTG	32860417	POW
Helgren, Elmer S.	S/Sgt, LWG	36408867	POW
Smith, Joseph F. III	Cpl, RWG	13080214	POW
Crowe, Arthur E. Jr.	S/Sgt, TG	11063947	POW

STATEMENT BY S/SGT. THOMAS R. WILEY, 18208488

The formation was attacked by FW-190s and ME-109s. Aircraft B-17G, serial number 42-97209 sustained damage to the right wing. Several large holes appeared and gas started leaking over the wing. The aircraft pulled out of formation and joined the group ahead, apparently still under control. The group which aircraft 42-97209 joined was seemingly a miscellaneous assortment of ships from different groups flying together after enemy fighters had broken the original formations.

12 MAY 1944, 8TH AF, 452ND BG, 728TH BS

Target: Brux (Most), Czechoslovakia
Aircraft type, model and series: B-17G, Serial No. 42-97864
Engine - type, model and series: R-1820-97
Engines Nos. (a) SW-013175 (b) SW-012463 (c) SW-013254 (d) SW-013268
Nickname of aircraft: Unknown
Type of mission: Bombing
Aircraft was lost as result of enemy aircraft. Last seen at 1220 hours approximately at 50/17 N, 07/40 E.
Point of departure: AAF STA 142

CREW POSITION, NAME IN FULL

Patrick, Robert C.	Capt, Pilot	0-432641	POW
Kerr, Robert F.	1st Lt, Copilot	0-790472	POW
McCracken, John H. Jr.	2nd Lt, Nav.	0-707082	POW
Lewis, Thomas J. Jr.	2nd Lt, Bomb.	0-757726	POW

Herwig, John D.	Sgt, TTG	38367571	POW
Otte, Theodore C. Jr.	Sgt, RO	38396609	POW
Jones, Harrie Jr.	Sgt, BTG	39696800	POW
Sherrell, Millard H.	Sgt, LWG	34710708	POW
Cadle, Joseph P.	Sgt, RWG	34763130	POW
Woods, Edmond A.	Sgt, TG	35022995	POW

STATEMENT BY S/SGT. THOMAS R. WILEY, 18208488

The formation was attacked by FW-190s and ME-109s. On the first pass aircraft B-17G, Serial No. 42-97864 was hit and number four engine caught fire. It looked as though the engine was melting off the right horizontal stabilizer. The aircraft stayed in formation despite this difficulty. The enemy aircraft made a second pass. Fire appeared in the waist of aircraft No. 42-97864 and it pulled out of formation. When last observed the aircraft was going down out of control.

Approximately 75 parachutes were observed in the general vicinity as the fighters attacked in large numbers and knocked out quite a few ships.

12 MAY 1944, 8TH AF, 452ND BG, 729TH BS

Target: Brux (Most), Czechoslovakia
Aircraft type, model and series: B-17G, Serial No. 42-97235
Engine - type, model and series: R-1820-97
Engines Nos. (a) SW-013350 (b) SW-013419 (c) SW-013307 (d) SW-007181
Nickname of aircraft: Unknown
Type of mission: Bombing
Aircraft was lost as a result of enemy aircraft. Last seen at 1220 hours approximately at 50/17 N, 07/40 E
Point of departure: AAF STA 142

CREW POSITION, NAME IN FULL

Naylor, Walter V.	2nd Lt, Pilot	0-753238	KIA
Carpenter, Winecke F.	2nd Lt, Copilot	0-699795	POW
Casselberry, Austin F.	2nd Lt, Nav.	0-707855	KIA
Veselich, Michael M.	2nd Lt, Bomb	0-757932	KIA
Mullenmeister, Roger J.	S/Sgt, TTG	17109777	POW
Mitchell, Duward F.	S/Sgt, RO	38340264	KIA
Ahern, John W.	Sgt, BTG	37159083	KIA
Berkoben, Richard R.	Sgt, RWG	12095281	POW
Garten, Thomas G.	Sgt, LWG	15394434	POW
Bates, Ralph R.	Sgt, TG	39408809	POW

STATEMENT BY T/SGT. THOMAS G. GARTEN, 15394434

Our aircraft left formation over Frankfurt, Germany. We were hit by enemy fighters and I was blown out of ship. Our ship struck the ground near Frankfurt. Following members of crew were in the aircraft when it struck the ground: 2nd Lt. Veselich, 2nd Lt. Casselberry, Sgt. Ahern and S/Sgt. Mitchell.

2ND LT. WALTER V. NAYLOR 0-753238

2nd Lt. Naylor bailed out near Frankfurt, Germany. He was not injured. Last contact on interphone before being attacked by fighters. Last seen in pilots seat. I was told by Copilot 2nd Lt. Carpenter that Pilot 2nd Lt. Naylor hit No. 2 prop. in act of bailing out. Chute did not blossom.

2ND LT. WINECKE F. CARPENTER, 0-699795

2nd Lt. Carpenter bailed out near Frankfurt, Germany. Last contact before attack.

2ND LT. AUSTIN F. CASSELBERRY, 0-707855

2nd Lt. Casselberry did not bail out. Last contact during attack from one o'clock by fighters. Last seen in nose of ship. It was impossible for him to bail out. Our ship went into flat spin and he was held in ship by centrifugal force.

2ND LT. MICHAEL M. VESELICH, 0-757932

2nd Lt. Veselich did not bail out. He was stuck in nose of ship and went down with ship.

S/SGT. DUWARD F. MITCHELL, 38340264

S/Sgt. Mitchell did not bail out. He was trapped in radio room. It was impossible for him to bail out, because we still had bomb load. No escape hatch.

SGT. JOHN W. AHERN, 37159083

Sgt. Ahern did not bail out. He could not operate ball turret because electrical system was shot out. Sgt. Ahern didn't have time to operate hand cranks. It was impossible to bail out!

12 MAY 1944, 8TH AF, 388TH BG, 561ST BS

Target: Brux (Most), Czechoslovakia
Aircraft type, model and series: B-17G, Serial No. 42-31549
Engine - type, model and series: R-1820-97
Engine Nos. (a) 42-138381 (b) SW-012231 (c) 43-62760 (d) SW-005009
Nickname of aircraft: Unknown
Type of mission: Bombing
Aircraft was lost as a result of enemy aircraft. Last seen at 1238 hours approximately at 50/25 N, 08/40 E.
Point of departure: AAF STA 136

CREW POSITION, NAME IN FULL

Loslo, Alex	2nd Lt, Pilot	0-690127	POW
Wilson, Robert S.	2nd Lt, Copilot	0-819026	POW
Morrison, Douglas B.	Nav.	0-706954	POW
Philips, Presley E.	2nd Lt, Bomb.	0-757913	POW
Veronica, William J.	S/Sgt, RO	32130340	POW
Seiter, Albert E. Jr.	S/Sgt, Eng TTG	35470977	POW
Durling, Clarence F.	Sgt, BTG	32837979	POW
Regan, George F.	Sgt, LWG	11065584	POW
Jones, Archie E.	Sgt, RWG	34539001	POW
Spinella, Caraine J.	Sgt, TG	32806733	POW

Report On Shot-Down American Aircraft

Date and time aircraft was shot-down: 12 May 1944 at 1245 hours
Place of crash: Stannheim, District of Friedberg, Germany.
Type of aircraft: Boeing B-17G
Markings: American decal on both sides of the fuselage, in yellow sign "Allie" and 13 bombs in yellow paint. On the tail assembly in yellow paint number 231549 under this a "A."
Place of crash: Aircraft lies at the limits of the town on a pasture field, scattered in a distance of 500 meters.
Condition of aircraft: Aircraft blew up in the air, left engine destroyed and is scattered in a distance of 500 meters. Engines are dug into the crash crater.
Weapons: 12 machine guns found, six of the machine guns are damaged
Bombs: Thirty 100 pounds bombs found, they were defused.
Information on downing— statement by mayor: The left out board engine burning while the aircraft was approaching. Aircraft lost altitude and when it was about 300 meters high a darting flame came out of the aircraft and following explosion tore the aircraft to pieces.
Disposition of crew: 10 men captured.

12 May 1944, 8th AF, 452nd BG, 728th BS

Target: Brux (Most), Czechoslovakia
Aircraft type, model and series: B-17G, Serial No. 42-31345
Engine - type, model and series: R-1820-97
Engine Nos. (a) SW-004738 (b) SW-006022 (c) 43-60469 (d) SW-31345
Nickname of aircraft: Unknown
Type of mission: Bombing
Point of departure: AAF STA 142

Crew position, name in full

Orcutt, Merl D.	S/Sgt, TTG	38394689	KIA

Statement By F/O Harold Eastman Jr., T-61908

During an attack by enemy fighters S/Sgt. Orcutt was struck in the head by fire from 20mm cannon and died instantly. Returning from the mission it was necessary to ditch in the English Channel. The body went down with the ship as the crew was unable to remove it before the ship sank. The approximate location of the ship when sinking occurred was 1-1/2 miles west of Knockfortjohn, Kent County, England, in Channel.

12 May 1944, 8th AF, 95th BG, 336th BS

Target: Brux (Most), Czechoslovakia
Aircraft type, model and series: B-17G, Serial No. 42-39884
Engine - type, model and series: R-1820-97
Nickname of aircraft: Unknown
Type of mission: Bombing. Aircraft was last seen near Ostende, Belgium. Aircraft was lost for unknown reason.
Point of departure: AAF STA 119

Part of the crew, back row l-r: Sgt. Paul F. Newman, 2nd Lt. Val F. Humme, 2nd Lt. Walter L. Corrigan, S/Sgt. Richard M. Harbeck, Sgt. Genuvino V. Di Mayo. Front row l-r: Sgt. Loris R. Smith, S/Sgt. Charles R. Lyon, Sgt. Marcus B. Cullum.

CREW POSITION, NAME IN FULL

Yablonowski, Edwin M.	2nd Lt, Pilot	0-813100	KIA
Corrigan, Walter L.	2nd Lt, Copilot	0-819253	KIA
Madigan, John F. Jr.	2nd Lt, Nav.	0-809696	KIA
Humme, Val F.	2nd Lt, Bomb.	0-701479	KIA
Harbeck, Richard M.	S/Sgt, ROG	32830742	POW
Lyon, Charles R.	S/Sgt, TTG	15354744	KIA
Di Mayo, Genuvino V.	Sgt, BTG	36048521	POW
Newman, Paul F.	Sgt, RWG	13111854	KIA
Smith, Loris R.	Sgt, LWG	12174302	KIA
Cullum, Marcus B.	Sgt, TG	18219415	KIA

STATEMENT BY T/SGT. RICHARD M. HARBECK, 32830742

Our aircraft left formation I believe over south central Germany. Two men of our crew bailed out. I was the first to leave the ship through the waist door. I had tripped over something and had fallen directly in front of the open escape hatch. I had to get out in a hurry so that the others could get out. Someone helped to shove me out. I do not know however who that person was. I landed someplace several miles south of Frankfurt, Germany, but because I was transported in such a manner as not to be able to see the names of any towns upon my capture, I cannot locate the area.

L-R: Sgt. Loris R. Smith, S/Sgt. Richard M. Harbeck, 2nd Lt. Edwin M. Yablonovski

2nd Lt. Edwin M. Yablonowski	O-813100
2nd Lt. Walter L. Corrigan	O-819253
2nd Lt. John F. Madigan Jr.	O-809696
2nd Lt. Val F. Humme	O-701479
S/Sgt. Charles R. Lyon	15354744
Sgt. Paul F. Newman	13111854
Sgt. Marcus B. Cullum	18219415
Sgt. Loris R. Smith	12174302

I don't know, if any of these members of our crew bailed out, but I doubt it. I am quite certain that I saw our aircraft explode almost immediately after I bailed out.

Capt. Ed Onze, a very close friend of 2nd Lt. Edwin M. Yablonowski, and his family visited the site in Germany where 2nd Lt. Yablonowski landed his aircraft. Capt. Onze also photographed the immediate area of the incident with photos showing the cemetery where Germans buried members of the crew killed in bomb blast from bombs carried on board. The B-17G exploded in the town of Rod on the Weil River, which is 20 miles north northwest of Frankfurt on Main, Germany. Capt. Onze was killed in action during the Korean War.

12 MAY 1944, 8TH AF, 452ND BG, 730TH BS

Target: Brux (Most), Czechoslovakia
Aircraft type, model and series: B-17G, Serial No. 42-37947
Engine - type, model and series: R-1820-97

Capt. Ed Onze, 160th Recon Squadron Photo (JP)

2nd Lt. Edwin M. Yablonowski and his comrades in grave 2930-3, Section 34, Arlington National Cemetery, Fort Myer, VA

View of cemetery in which the Germans buried the bodies. It's on a very steep hill. The house of the man who was Burgomaster at the time of the accident is also in picture.

General view of south side of Rod.

This was taken from the direction in which Ed brought his plane down. The cemetery is on the other side of the woods.

2nd Lt. Bruce Davis

L-R: S/Sgt. Arthur H. Mills, S/Sgt. Richard H. Jeffries

L-R: S/Sgt. Arthur H. Mills, Sgt. William G, Woodruff

S/Sgt. Arthur H. Mills

L-R: 2nd Lt. Bruce Davis, 2nd Lt. Truman L. Manning, 2nd Lt. David H. Foust

Engine Nos., (a) SW-866 (b) SW-869 (c) SW-876 (d) SW-638
Nickname of aircraft: Unknown
Type of mission: Bombing
Aircraft was lost as a result of enemy aircraft. Last seen between Koblenz and Frankfurt, Germany. No further information available on this ship due to the confusion existing at the time of enemy attacks.
Point of departure: AAF STA 142

CREW POSITION, NAME IN FULL

Davis, Bruce	2nd Lt, Pilot	0-462203	POW	Dulag Luft
Manning, Truman L.	2nd Lt, Copilot	0-760641	POW	Dulag Luft
Foust, David H.	2nd Lt, Nav	0-707888	POW	Dulag Luft
Sundborg, John C.	2nd Lt, Bomb	0-683098	POW	Dulag Luft
Mills, Arthur H.	SSgt/TTG	13060829	POW	Dulag Luft
Jeffries, Richard H.	SSgt/RO	33463274	POW	Dulag Luft
Sable, Richard V.	Sgt/BTG	16098170	POW	Dulag Luft
Woodruff, William G.	Sgt/RWG	18191975	POW	Dulag Luft
Brawley, Dewey F.	Sgt/LWG	39124417	POW	Dulag Luft
Conniff, Donald O.	Sgt/TG	39284465	POW	Dulag Luft

Date and time aircraft was shot-down: 12 May 1944 at 1300 hours. 7-1/2 km northeast of Aschaffenburg, Mainfranken.

Kind of capture: fighter aircraft
Type of aircraft: B-17, Fortress

12 MAY 1944, 8TH AF, 452ND BG, 730TH BS

Target: Brux (Most), Czechoslovakia
Aircraft type, model and series: B-17G, Serial No. 42-39902
Engine - type, model and series: R-1820-97
Nickname of aircraft: Unknown
Aircraft not lost
Point of departure: AAF STA 142

CREW POSITION, NAME IN FULL

Denham, William E.	1st Lt, Pilot	0-745642	RTD
Krout, Robert T.	2nd Lt, Copilot	0-754432	RTD
Van Hersett, George E.	1st Lt, Nav.	0-692099	RTD
McCready, Robert O.	1st Lt, Bomb.	0-753149	RTD
Kulbacki, Bernard B.	T/Sgt, TTG	13158094	RTD
McHardy, Bryson R.	T/Sgt, RO	17156029	RTD
Scarpone, Anthony M.	S/Sgt, BTG	32534086	RTD
Harmon, Clarence B.	S/Sgt, RWG	14160803	MIA*
Sabo, Charles M.	S/Sgt, LWG	33572781	RTD
Stanberry, Willie	S/Sgt, TG	38447430	RTD

*Bailed out over target. The other nine crew members returned to England in aircraft B-17G, Serial No. 42-39902

Back Row, l-r: 2nd Lt. William E. Thompson, 2nd Lt. Leonard Eichenbaum, 2nd Lt. Claude C. Martin. Front Row: S/Sgt. Michael Kutaga, S/Sgt. Henry Pruett, S/Sgt. Lawrence J. Laurie, S/Sgt. Jack N. Kimble, T/Sgt. Robert E. Pinneo, T/Sgt. Jon Niechniedovicz

STATEMENT BY 1ST LT. WILLIAM E. DENHAM, 0-745642

The Right Waist Gunner, S/Sgt. Clarence B. Harmon, 14160803, bailed out on way back (50/25 N, 12/50 E). The pilot stated that "Everything was salvoed, guns were out, gunner misunderstood and thought instructions were to bail out. Crew had been instructed to put on chutes. This gunner was working on ball turret. I gave the order to jump and this gunner, being the nerviest of the crew and trying to make it easier for the rest of them, misunderstood and jumped believing that his actions would reassure the men to follow."

12 MAY 1944, 8TH AF, 452ND BG, 791ST BS

Target: Brux (Most), Czechoslovakia
Aircraft type, model and series: B-17G, Serial No. 42-39976
Engines - type, model and series: R-1820-97
Engines Nos. (a) SW-180 (b) SW-205 (c) SW-002303 (d) SW-238
Nickname of aircraft: Unknown
Type of mission: Bombing
Aircraft was lost as a result of mechanical difficulty. Last seen at 1400 hours at approximately 50/13 N, 13/39 E.
Point of departure: AAF STA 142

CREW POSITION, NAME IN FULL

Martin, Claude C.	2nd Lt, Pilot	0-809836	POW
Eichenbaum, Leonard	2nd Lt, Copilot	0-818650	POW
Miller, Ward K.	2nd Lt, Nav.	0-703124	POW
Thompson, William E.	2nd Lt, Bomb.	0-756928	POW
Niechniedowicz, John	T/Sgt, TTG	32710744	POW
Kutaga, Michael	S/Sgt, RWG	31148134	POW
Pinneo, Robert E.	T/Sgt, RO	36614378	POW
Laurie, Lawrence J.	S/Sgt, LWG	36046250	POW
Kimble, Jack N.	S/Sgt, BTG	34601765	POW
Pruett, Henry	S/Sgt, TG	17121889	POW

REPORT ON SHOT-DOWN AMERICAN AIRCRAFT

Date and time aircraft was shot-down: 12 May 1944 at approximately 1439 hours
Place of crash: 2 km northwest of Koengen, Esslingen County, 20 km southeast of Stuttgart
Type of aircraft: B-17G, Fortress
Kind of capture: Presumably by fighter
Condition of aircraft: Hit right outer power plant, presumably resulting from fighter fire. Fuselage and wings show several minor perforations, probably caused by AA fire fragments. Findings on bottom are pending, because aircraft landed on belly. Aircraft is well preserved. Slightly damaged by belly landing. Total damage 20%.

Damages: Left and right inner engine mountings slightly squashed, bottom of fuselage damaged by crash. Several damages resulting from flak fragments at fuselage, wings and tail assembly. Ball Turret damaged at fuselage. Green house squashed and damaged by crash. All plants and installations (navigational equipment, armament and radio) are well preserved and in operating condition,

Crew: 10 men crew captured at landing point at 1440 hours.

12 MAY 1944, 8TH AF, 452ND BG, 728TH BS

Target: Brux (Most), Czechoslovakia
Aircraft type, model and series: B-17G, Serial No. 42-97361

Engines - type, model and series: R-1820-97
Nickname of aircraft: Unknown
Type of mission: Bombing
Aircraft last seen at 1222 hours approximately at 50/17 N, 07/40 E.
Point of departure: AAF STA 142

CREW POSITION, NAME IN FULL

Halbleib, Alexander J.	2nd Lt, Pilot	0-810873	POW
Kelly, George B.	F/O, Copilot	T-61935	POW
Kniffen, Samuel K.	F/O, Nav.	T-124489	POW
Shulman, Charles H.	2nd Lt, Bomb.	0-757750	POW
Binkele, Edward R.	S/Sgt, TTG	36447640	POW
Carr, Joseph F.	S/Sgt, RO	13079481	KIA
Nader, Francis J.	Sgt, BTG	19167909	KIA
Morgan, Willard D.	Sgt, LWG	34681225	KIA
Postelwaite, Wilbur F.	Sgt, RWG	35597985	POW
McDonough, Patrick J.	Sgt, TG	31304550	KIA

REPORT ON SHOT-DOWN AMERICAN AIRCRAFT

Date and time aircraft was shot-down: 12 May 1944 about 1230 hours
Place of crash: 2 km southeast Ohren, County Limburg
Kind of capture: Fighter
Type of aircraft: B-17G
Condition of aircraft: The aircraft was hit in the air by fighter and blew up into pieces. Fuselage, wings, tail assembly and engines were destroyed completely.
Crew: Sgt. Patrick J. McDonough, 31304550, dead. Six other members of the crew were unidentifiable and buried in the community cemetery at Ohren, county of Limburg. Only four dead on Sgt. McDonough crew.

STATEMENT BY T/SGT. EDWARD R. BINKELE, 36447640

Our aircraft left formation East of Frankfurt, one hour from target. Our ship was hit fast and hard and went in a sharp spinning dive, controls out.

Bail out order given by pilot. I was off intercom. fighting fire and smoke in top turret vicinity and bomb bay. Not hearing bail out signal, I was last to leave in nose and cockpit. All made it there. Our ship circled me while in chute. I could see our Right Waist Gunner Sgt. Postelwaite trying to bail out the waist door from the diving aircraft. He made it very close to the ground.

A second later the aircraft crashed. I think his story will say that he was the first and only man in the waist to jump, I saw no one bail out after him. I lost track of aircraft when it appeared to be only 1,000 feet off the ground. That is the chance these four men had. The aircraft was in 60 degree dive and right spin, making it very hard for them. This information of mine is as definite as might be possible. After screening all general and precise information from my crew members remaining and while in Germany it is without much doubt that these four men were killed in action on 12 May 1944:
S/Sgt. Joseph F. Carr, 13079481
Sgt. Francis J. Nader, 19167909
Sgt. Willard D. Morgan, 34681225
Sgt. Patrick J. McDonough, 31304550

12 MAY 1944, 8TH AF, 452ND BG, 730TH BS

Target: Brux (Most), Czechoslovakia

Aircraft type, model and series: B-17G, Serial No. 42-39937
Engines - type, model and series: R-1820-97
Engines Nos. (a) 43-65352 (b) 43-65367 (c) 41-56747 (d) 43-56985
Nickname of aircraft: Unknown
Type of mission: Bombing
Aircraft last seen between Koblenz and Frankfurt, Germany. Aircraft was lost as a result of enemy aircraft.
Point of departure: AAF, STA 142

Crew position, name in full

Hemer, Harold H.	2nd Lt, Pilot	0-749692	KIA
Canterbury, Charles L. Jr.	2nd Lt, Copilot	0-755278	KIA
Longenecker, Robert T.	2nd Lt, Nav.	0-752688	KIA
Zell, Edward J.	S/Sgt, Bomb.	33481673	KIA
Carnes, Raymond C.	S/Sgt, TTG	18199695	DOI
Baumgardner, William J.	S/Sgt, RO	33031042	POW
Griffith, Thomas M.	Sgt, BTG	35652036	POW
Michaud, Elmer J.	Pvt, LWG	31283332	POW
Bethune, Norman P.	Sgt, RWG	11037848	POW
Dickey, Roy D.	Sgt, TG	33574228	POW

Report On Shot-Down American Aircraft

Date and time aircraft was shot-down: 12 May 1944 at 1520 hours
Place of crash: The hill, 4 km southeast of Rudersdorf, Siegen County
Kind of capture: Crash landing
Type of aircraft: B-17G Fortress
Markings of aircraft: In white square spot letter L, below Letter G
Following four American airmen, killed in action were buried at the cemetery of Rudersdorf District Siegen on 13 May 1944 at 1630 hours.

Name and Rank	Grave Location
2nd Lt. Charles L. Canterbury	Section 7, 3rd row, grave No. 3.
Sgt. Edward J. Zell	Section 7, 3rd row, grave No. 2.
2nd Lt. Robert T. Longenecker	Section 7, 3rd row, grave No. 1.
2nd Lt. Harold H. Hemer	Section 7, 3rd row, grave No. 4.

12 May 1944, 8th AF, 452nd BG, 731st BS

Target, Brux (Most), Czechoslovakia
Aircraft type, model and series: B-17G, Serial No. 42-39941
Engines - type, model and series: R-1820-97
Engines Nos. (a) 43-66308 (b) 43-66310 (c) SW-005967 (d) 43-66338
Nickname of aircraft. Unknown
Type of mission: Bombing
Aircraft last seen at 1525 hours approximately at 50/25 N, 06/47 E.
Point of departure: AAF STA 142

Crew position, name in full

Noble, Richard F.	2nd Lt, Pilot	0-453171	Evaded/MIA
Viafore, Daniel G.	2nd Lt, Copilot	0-818248	Evaded
Laule, Richard D.	2nd Lt Nav.	0-700741	Evaded/POW

Clago, Bruce W.	2nd Lt, Bomb.	0-749756	Evaded/POW
Martin, Lloyd A.	S/Sgt, TTG	33430645	Evaded/POW
Atkins, Robert	T/Sgt, RO	32792318	Evaded
Moody, Vernon L.	S/Sgt, RWG	37344164	POW
Brush, George V.	S/Sgt, LWG	32229463	POW
Munn, Ralph J.	S/Sgt, BTG	39555640	Evaded/POW
Davies, Leon H.	S/Sgt, TG	39246153	POW

STATEMENT BY 1ST LT. RAYMOND KURTZ, 0-1042858

After leaving the target aircraft Ser. No. 42-39941 called for fighter support. He had an engine out but the aircraft was under control. Nearing Frankfurt, Germany he called on "A" channel saying "I don't think I'll make the coast." 1 told him to hang on if possible until friendly occupied territory was reached and then bail out his crew, His last word was "Roger, will try to make it." Last seen on course straggling.

STATEMENT BY 1ST LT. DONALD W. HATTREM, 0-677732

Aircraft B-17G, Ser. No. 42-39941 was hit by flak directly over Brux, Czechoslovakia. With two engines out it dropped out of formation and fell behind. The pilot called me for fighter protection and I called the fighters. Fighter support arrived in about five minutes. When last seen A/C 941 was straggling far behind the formation, almost at the border of France, on course and under control.

12 MAY 1944, 8TH AF, 452ND BG, 729TH BS

Target: Brux (Most), Czechoslovakia
Aircraft type, model and series: B-17G, Serial No. 42-97786
Engines - type, model and series: R-1820-97
Engines Nos. (a) SW-011131 (b) SW-011150 (c) SW-011197 (d) SW-011053
Nickname of aircraft: Unknown
Type of mission: Bombing. Aircraft last seen at 1220 hours at approximately 50/17 N, 07/40 E
Point of Departure: AAF STA 142

CREW POSITION, NAME IN FULL

Thomas, Joseph C.	1st Lt, Pilot	0-803308	murdered on the ground by Germans
Rose, Adrian W.	2nd Lt Copilot	0-691061	POW
Holley, Harold R.	2nd Lt Nav.	0-692404	POW
Millsap, James W.	2nd Lt Bomb.	0-681783	murdered on the ground by Germans
Strom, William R.	S/Sgt, TTG	36223536	POW
Wolfe, Maxwell	S/Sgt, RO	32780613	POW
Hall, William E.	Pvt, BTG	12044761	KIA
Fisher, Arnold L.	S/Sgt, LWG	18209594	POW
Owens, James E.	S/Sgt, RWG	38341598	POW
Myers, Robert C.	S/Sgt, TG	39283218	KIA

STATEMENT BY S/SGT. JAMES E. OWENS, 38341598

Our aircraft left formation near Koblenz, Germany. S/Sgt. Arnold L. Fisher and S/Sgt. Maxwell Wolfe bailed out the waist door before I did. Tail Gunner S/Sgt. Robert C. Myers was killed before I bailed out. Ball Turret Gunner Pvt. William E. Hall and Tail Gunner S/Sgt. Robert C. Myers were in the aircraft when it struck the ground near Koblenz, Germany.

Crew of "Hairless Joe" B-17G, Serial No. 42-97371. Front row, l-r: 2nd Lt. James T. Lundebjerg, 2nd Lt. Ralph G. Scott, 2nd Lt. Hugh T. Atkinson. Back row, l-r: S/Sgt. John W. Covill, Sgt. Donald H. Jones, Sgt. Bob G. Johnson, Sgt. Edward K. Brown Jr., Sgt. Jack L. Nelson, S/Sgt. Ervin A. Nordt. Photograph taken in January 1944 at Pyote, TX, ready for overseas flight.

Pilot 1st Lt. Joseph C. Thomas, 0-803308, bailed out near Koblenz. I believe he was killed by Germans on the ground.

Bomb. 2nd Lt. James W, Millsap, 0-681783, bailed out near Koblenz. I believe he was killed by Germans on the ground.

Tail Gunner S/Sgt. Robert C. Myers, 39283218, did not bail out. He was seen dead in tail position.

12 MAY 1944, 8TH AF, 452ND BG, 728TH BS

Target: Brux (Most), Czechoslovakia
Aircraft type, model and series: B-17G, Serial No. 42-97371
Engines - type, model and series: R-1820-97
Engines Nos. (a) SW-009844 (b) SW-009800 (c) SW-009916 (d) SW-009924
Nickname of aircraft: Unknown
Type of mission: Bombing
Aircraft last seen at 1220 hours approximately at 50/17 N, 07/40 E.
Point of departure: AAF STA 142

CREW

Atkinson, Hugh Talmadge	2nd Lt	0-750763	Captured Dulag Luft
Lundebjerg, James T.	2nd Lt	0-703028	Captured Dulag Luft

S/Sgt. Erwin A. Nord

Headley, Francis Lee	2nd Lt	0-689154	Captured Dulag Luft
Scott, Ralph C.	2nd Lt	0-760517	Captured Dulag Luft
Nordt, Ervin Albert	S/Sgt	18118685	Captured Dulag Luft
Johnson, Bob Guy	Sgt	35549817	Captured Dulag Luft
Jones, Donald Harvey	Sgt	35605202	Captured Dulag Luft
Covill, John William	S/Sgt	36049098	Captured Dulag Luft
Brown, Edward Keyes	Sgt	32237535	Captured Dulag Luft
Nelson, Jack Lester	Sgt	18046366	Captured Dulag Luft

REPORT ON SHOT-DOWN AMERICAN AIRCRAFT

Date and time aircraft was shot-down: 12 May 1944 at 1230 hours
Place of crash: Echzell, county of Buedingen
Type of aircraft: B-17 Fortress
Condition of aircraft: 95% destruction
Markings: L at square 2973

12 MAY 1944, 8TH AF, 96TH BG 339TH BS

Target: Brux (Most), Czechoslovakia
Aircraft type, model and series: B-17G, Serial No. 42-107189
Engines - type, model and series: R-1820-97

Engine Nos. (a) SW-011504 (b) SW-014104 (c) SW-014266 (d) SW-013984
Nickname of aircraft: Unknown
Type of mission: Bombing
Aircraft was lost as a result of enemy aircraft. Last seen at 1210 hours approximately at 50/10 N, 07/10 E.
Point of departure: AAF STA 138

CREW POSITION, NAME IN FULL

Simons, Robert W.	1st Lt, Pilot	0-803700	KIA
Duncan, Horace K.	1st Lt, Copilot	0-751727	KIA
Nelson, Garnett O.	2nd Lt, Nav.	0-706957	KIA
Russell, Jack R.	1st Lt, Bomb.	0-746615	KIA
Paul, Harland B.	T/Sgt, Eng. TT	19123287	KIA
Keshel, Walter J.	T/Sgt, RORG	16155388	KIA
Petrosky, Joseph R.	S/Sgt, Asst. Eng. RW	33439022	KIA
Russo, Anthony N.	S/Sgt, Asst. ROBT	32507542	KIA
Wethor, John M.	S/Sgt, TG	37548031	POW
Good, Ralph E., Jr.	S/Sgt, LW	11100543	KIA

1st Lt. Eugene F. Aldridge, Netherlands American Military Cemetery, Margraten, Holland, Plot E, Row 9, Grave 25

12 MAY 1944, 8TH AF, 96TH BG, 339TH BS

Target: Brux (Most), Czechoslovakia
Aircraft type, model and series: B-17G, Serial No. 42-102571
Engines - type, model and series: R-1820-97
Engine Nos. (a) SW-010710 (b) SW-015678 (c) SW-010867 (d) 43-64156
Nickname of aircraft: Unknown
Type of mission: Bombing
Aircraft was lost as a result of enemy aircraft. Aircraft last known position at 50/10 N, 07/10 E.
Point of departure: AAF STA 138

CREW POSITION, NAME IN FULL

Laurie, Robert H.	1st Lt, Pilot	0-753899	KIA
Rengers, Leo B.	2nd Lt, Copilot	0-815235	KIA
Jones, Clifford D.	2nd Lt, Nav.	0-514329	POW
Little, Robert M.	2nd Lt, Bomb.	0-757532	KIA
Whitman, William H.	T/Sgt, Eng. TT	38396292	KIA
Henderson, Preston R.	T/Sgt, RORG	19177576	KIA
Kohan, Albert B.	S/Sgt, Asst. Eng. RW	33419044	KIA
Stone, Fred S.	S/Sgt, Asst. ROBT	12134896	KIA
Lanham, Lewis A.	S/Sgt, TG	16073859	POW
Corwin, Robert J.	S/Sgt, LW	35368283	KIA

STATEMENT BY 1ST LT. CLIFFORD D. JONES, 0-514329

At approximately 1245 hours at altitude 21,000 feet we were attacked by fighters. When our ship blew up I learned that tail gunner S/Sgt. Lanham was blown out the tail of the ship and was lucky in being conscious enough to pull the rip cord. I, as navigator, escaped through the nose hatch. I assume that the eight missing members of my crew were trapped in the ship and consequently died in the crash.

My first three days down I was quartered in a Catholic civilian hospital at Kamberg, Germany where I met a priest who could speak broken English. His name was Casper Hauptman and I feel certain he as well as the towns chief of police can straighten out with regard to the fate of my other crew members. I understand from him that there were about six bombers shot-down in that general area.

12 MAY 1944, 8TH AF, 96TH BG, 413TH BS

Target: Brux (Most), Czechoslovakia
Aircraft type, model and series: B-17G, Serial No. 42-97654
Engines - type, model and series: R-1820-97
Engine Nos. (a) 43-66286 (b) SW-007114 (c) SW-007112 (d) SW-007188
Nickname of aircraft: Unknown
Type of mission: Bombing
Aircraft was lost as a result of enemy aircraft. Last seen at 1210 hours approximately 50/20 N, 08/20 E. Aircraft on fire.
Point of departure: AAF STA 138

CREW POSITION, NAME IN FULL

Knupp, James E.	Capt, Pilot	0-661944	POW
Aldridge, Eugene F.	1st Lt, Copilot	0-687521	KIA

Lemley, Marcus J.	Lt Col, CP	0-1699161	KIA
Schultz, Chester J.	2nd Lt, Nav.	0-2045244	KIA
Helderman, Max A.	1st Lt, Bomb.	0-686086	KIA
Melgin, Irvin M.	1st Lt, Mickey Operator	0-672958	KIA
Waters, Dorcy W.	T/Sgt, Eng. TT	35338763	KIA
Ruben, Manuel	T/Sgt, RORG	13124775	POW
Emory, John R.	S/Sgt, Asst. Eng. RW	35420954	KIA
Cannon, William F. Jr.	S/Sgt, Asst. ROTG	38236783	KIA

12 MAY 1944, 8TH AF, 96TH BG, 337TH BS

Target: Brux (Most), Czechoslovakia
Aircraft type, model and series: B-17G, Serial No. 42-97567
Engines - type, model and series: R-1820-97
Engine Nos. (a) SW-007702 (b) SW-007914 (c) SW-007932 (d) SW-007974
Nickname of aircraft: Unknown
Type of mission. Bombing
Aircraft was lost as a result of enemy aircraft. Last seen at 1210 hours approximately 50/20 N, 08/20 E.
Point of departure: AAF STA 138

Netherlands American Military Cemetery, Margraten, Holland

CREW POSITION, NAME IN FULL

Moore, Thomas J.	1st Lt, Pilot	0-747465	KIA
Johnson, Victor P.	1st Lt, Copilot	0-697132	POW
Thomson, Richard W.	1st Lt, CP	0-672252	KIA
Williams, Norman E.	2nd Lt, Nav.	0-694905	KIA
Barber, William	2nd Lt, Bomb.	0-689514	KIA
Hall, Emery E.	2nd Lt, Mickey Operator	0-688037	POW
Packard, Harold J.	T/Sgt, Eng. TT	31228610	KIA
Hellstrom, Raymond C.	T/Sgt, RORG	16128166	POW
Krezer, Ruben E.	S/Sgt, Asst. ROBT	18191160	KIA
Brooks, Bernard L.	S/Sgt, Asst. Eng. RW	18047220	POW
Davenport, Oliver E.	S/Sgt, TG	39279592	KIA

STATEMENT BY 1ST LT. EMERY EDISON HALL, 0-688037

Our aircraft left formation over Erbach approximately 17 miles north of Frankfurt, Germany. I and three other crew members bailed out (T/Sgt. Hellstrom, 1st Lt. Johnson and S/Sgt. Brooks.) Our aircraft struck the ground just west of Erbach, Germany.

1ST LT. THOMAS J. MOORE, 0-747465

1st Lt. Moore did not bail out. We were hit by German fighters over Erbach at 1210 hours. The pilot's compartment was ripped apart. At 1215 hours I looked forward through the bomb-bays and saw 1st Lt. Moore slumped over on 1st Lt. Thomson's body. The compartment was one mass of twisted metal.

1ST LT. RICHARD W. THOMSON, 0-672252

1st Lt. Thomson did not bail out. Last contact at 1200 noon when I talked with him. At 1215 hours I looked forward through bomb-bays and saw him slumped over on the dash board. The place was one mass of twisted metal.

2ND LT. NORMAN E. WILLIAMS, 0-694905

2nd Lt. Williams did not bail out. Last contact just before 1200 noon when we talked with each other. He checked in on course. 2nd Lt. Williams must have been hit by the fighter attack in the front. He was a deputy lead navigator on this mission and he would have tried to establish contact with me if he had not been killed. I don't see how he could have gotten out of the ship, even if alive, as it was going down in its spin.

2ND LT. WILLIAM BARBER, 0-689514

2nd Lt. Barber did not bail out. Last contact just prior 1200 noon. We checked in and every thing was O.K. "Red" must have been killed. He did not have a chance. The fighter attack came so fast and ripped us apart—the attack came from 1:00 high and cut across the nose of our ship. 2nd Lt. Barber "Red" was the type of a fellow that would have died at his guns. From the way the ship was going down in a spin nose down, he couldn't have gotten out if he had not been killed.

T/SGT. HAROLD J. PACKARD, 31228610

T/Sgt. Packard did not bail out. He was riddled by 20mm and killed. Last seen at base of his top turret. I looked through bomb bays before bailing out and Harold was crumpled on the floor of his turret. From the condition of his turret he could not have been alive.

S/Sgt. Ruben E. Krezer, 18191160

S/Sgt. Krezer did not bail out because his neck was broken in a fall caused by the convulsive motion of the ship in spin. He had evidently crashed against the roof of the aircraft and then had hit a full ammunition case. He was dying as I crawled by him. There was nothing I could do for him. I was the last to leave the ship alive. I got out at about 5,000 feet.

S/Sgt. Oliver E. Davenport, 39279592

S/Sgt. Davenport did not bail out. He was flying in the nose as gunner. When we were over Erbach, Germany our ship was badly hit in the front by enemy fighters. Nobody could have lived in that front it was a mass of twisted metal.

The radio and inter phone went dead after the first wave attack. I could get no word from the rest of the ship. Before I bailed out I took a last look forward from the radio room. The middle of the ship - pilot's compartment, etc, was a twisted mess where 20mm had made holes as big as my head.

I must presume the nose section was even worse.

12 May 1944, 8th AF, 96th BG, 337th BS

Target: Brux (Most), Czechoslovakia
Aircraft type, model and series: B-17G, Serial No. 42-102452
Engines - type, model and series: R-1820-97
Engine Nos.: (a) SW-013211 (b) SW-013224 (c) SW-013023 (d) SW-013240
Nickname of aircraft: Unknown
Type of mission: Bombing
Aircraft was lost as a result of mid-air collision with another aircraft (42-97382), both ships went down in flames. Last seen at 1210 hours approximately 50/20 N, 08/25 E.
Point of departure: AAF STA 138

Crew position, name in full

Moore, Herbert E.	2nd Lt, Pilot	0-813758	POW
Giesse, Billie G.	2nd Lt, Copilot	0-818140	POW
Saex, Irving G.	2nd Lt, Nav.	0-699250	KIA
McGlasson, Edward T.	2nd Lt, Bomb.	0-700108	KIA
Dranginis, Stanley G.	T/Sgt, Eng. TT	33617240	POW
Cassell, Donald W.	Pvt, RORG	32793689	POW
Miller, Willard C.	Pvt, Asst. Eng. RW	38185423	POW
Mertz, Theodore H.	Pvt, Asst. ROBT	16145014	POW
Medill, William R.	S/Sgt, TG	11099238	POW
Needham, Elton R.	Pvt, LW	18232254	POW

12 May 1944, 8th AF, 96th BG, 337th BS

Target: Brux (Most), Czechoslovakia
Aircraft type, model and series: B-17G, Serial No. 42-97382
Engines - type, model, series: R-1820-97
Engine Nos. (a) SW-013211 (b) SW-013229 (c) SW-013023 (d) SW-013240
Nickname of aircraft: Unknown
Type of mission: Bombing
Aircraft was lost as a result of mid-air collision with aircraft No. 42-102452 avoiding exploding aircraft due to enemy aircraft. Last seen at 1207 hours approximately 50/20 N, 08/25 E.
Point of departure: AAF STA 138

S/Sgt. Milford E. Andrews. Netherlands American Military Cemetery, Margraten, Holland, Plot M, Row 3, Grave 9.

CREW POSITION, NAME IN FULL

Hon, Arthur C.	1st Lt, Pilot	0-751738	KIA.
Rowles, Paul M.	2nd Lt, Copilot	0-818945	KIA
Bremer, Glenn A.	2nd Lt, Nav.	0-757766	KIA
Keane, Thomas J.	2nd Lt, Bomb.	0-756990	KIA
Haney, William I.	T/Sgt, Eng. TT	35277674	KIA
Long, David G.	T/Sgt, RORG	32547688	POW
Tams, Floyd	Sgt, Asst. Eng. RW	39025888	POW
La Prath, Edward	S/Sgt, Asst. ROBT	39555707	KIA
Weber, Raymond K.	S/Sgt, TG	15322419	KIA
Sickerott, Helimuth H.	S/Sgt, LW	33488246	POW

Bishop's Office
Patterson, NJ

19 Sep 1945

My Dear Mrs. Keane,

Under date of 7 May 1945, I received a communication from the Reverend Casper Hofman, a Roman Catholic priest, living in Camberg, Germany. In his letter he gives me detail concerning the passing of one who is very dear to you.

On 12 May 1944 an air combat took place over my native town of Camberg, where I am now living. Twenty-seven Americans were killed in this combat. They are buried in the cemetery of Camberg as Catholics. Please advise Mrs. T.J. Keane of the death of Thomas J. Keane 0-756990. He wore a Saint Christopher medal with the inscription: "I am a Catholic, in case of an accident kindly notify a priest." All have been in a common grave with a cross and inscription: "Here lie 27 American airmen who fell in air combat in the community of Camberg, 12 May 1944."

Next day after the air combat I said mass for all 27 airment without exception of faith. I gave the grave benediction and since, in every daily mass I have remembered them in the "Memento Prodefunctis." This fact may be a consolation for the next of kin with whom I express sympathy. I trust that this message may not be a source of renewing sorrow, but rather one of consolation.

With every good wish, I am respectfully your,
Thomas A. McLaughlin, Bishop of Paterson

12 MAY 1944, 8TH AF 96TH BG, 339TH BS

Target: Brux (Most), Czechoslovakia
Aircraft type, model and series: B-17G, Serial No. 42-97167
Engines - type, model and series: R-1820-97
Engine Nos. (a) SW-007808 (b) SW-007733 (c) SW-010957 (d) SW-010588
Nickname of aircraft: Unknown
Type of mission: Bombing
Aircraft was lost as a result of enemy aircraft. Aircraft last seen at 1210 hours approximately 50/20 N, 08/40 E.
Point of departure: AAF STA 138

CREW POSITION, NAME IN FULL

Link, Jack E.	Capt, Pilot	0-364458	KIA
Simmons, Erwin W.	2nd Lt, Copilot	0-815571	KIA
Rieckelman, Robert F.	2nd Lt, Nav.	0-703317	POW
Federman, Robert J.	1st Lt, Bomb.	0-755004	KIA

Walker, Herman	T/Sgt, Eng. TT	32718855	KIA
Royall, Richard J. Jr.,	T/Sgt, RORG	33225423	KIA.
Chopp, John	S/Sgt, Asst. Eng.	39199270	KIA
McGill, Clement F.	S/Sgt, Asst. ROBT	39120664	KIA
Burgess, Boyd R.	S/Sgt, TG	16057916	KIA
Andrews, Milford E.	S/Sgt, LW	38411591	KIA

REPORT ON SHOT-DOWN AMERICAN AIRCRAFT

Date and time aircraft was shot-down: 12 May 1944 at 1235 hours. Location of aircraft: Unterlahn/Limburg, Hahnstaetten County, Germany.

Type of aircraft: Fortress B-17G, Serial No. 297167.

Disposition of crew: nine dead.

12 MAY 1944, 8TH AF, 96TH BG, 337TH BS

Target: Brux (Most) Czechoslovakia

Aircraft type, model and series: B-17G, Serial No. 42-31718

Engines - type, model and series: R-1820-97

Engine Nos. (a) 43-60477 (b) SW-011498 (c) 41-41802 (d) 43-145805

Nickname of aircraft: Unknown

Type of mission: Bombing

Aircraft was lost as a result of enemy aircraft. Aircraft last seen at 1210 hours approximately 50/10 N, 07/10 E.

Point of departure: AAF STA 138

CREW POSITION, NAME IN FULL

Musser, Jerry T.	2nd Lt, Pilot	0-733961	POW
Simpson, Kenneth C.	2nd Lt, Copilot	0-809886	POW
Moore, Richard F., Jr.,	2nd Lt, Nav.	0-709432	KIA
Tice, Addison O.	2nd Lt, Bomb.	0-757858	POW
Gibbs, Finis R.	T/Sgt, Eng. TT	34508288	POW
Humphrey, Paul T.	T/Sgt, RORG	32143452	KIA
Fliegelman, Louis	S/Sgt, Asst. ROBT	13046100	POW
Reeves, Alfred H.	S/Sgt, Asst. Eng. RW	39038714	POW
Pearson, Robert D.	S/Sgt, TG	37307582	POW
Lewis, Glenn H.	S/Sgt, LW	11038219	POW

REPORT ON SHOT-DOWN AMERICAN AIRCRAFT

Date and time aircraft was shot-down: 12 May 1944 about 1300 hours

Disposition of crew: two men recovered dead; one, Paul T. Humphrey, interred at Hartmannshain.

Condition of aircraft: aircraft landed on grass, was set on fire by crew. Details of shooting down: According to witness report, aircraft was forced down by three fighters, hits in fuselage, fin by flak fragments.

Type of aircraft: B-17G, Serial No. 42-31718

At the fin black C in gray square, below in yellow: No. 231718, on fuselage, white T, both sides.

12 MAY 1944, 8TH AF, 96TH BG, 338TH BS

Target: Brux (Most), Czechoslovakia

Aircraft type, model and series: B-17G, Serial No. 42-31621

Engines - type, model and series: R-1820-97
Engine Nos. (a) 43-62135 (b) 43-145728 (c) 43-62964 (d) 42-138337
Nickname of aircraft: Unknown
Type of mission: Bombing
Aircraft was lost as a result of enemy aircraft. Aircraft last seen at 1210 hours approximately 50/10 N, 0710 E.
Point of departure: AAF STA 138

CREW POSITION, NAME IN FULL

Filer, Charles W.	2nd Lt, Pilot	0-810854	KIA
La Vigna, Fred K.	2nd Lt, Copilot	0-814918	KIA
Dink, John H.	2nd Lt, Nav.	0-707241	POW
Turcott, George L. Jr.	2nd Lt, Bomb.	0-756930	POW
Mochetti, Lido R.	T/Sgt, Eng.	31214993	KIA
Williams, Charles E.	T/Sgt, RORG	19095116	POW
Brogren, Carl E. Jr.	S/Sgt, Asst. Eng. RW	18214993	KIA
Pince, Charles V.	S/Sgt, Asst. ROBT	37559431	POW
Thornhill, Charles W.	S/Sgt TG	38372526	POW
Beck, Fred R.	S/Sgt, LW	34605802	KIA

STATEMENT BY S/SGT. CHARLES W. THORNHILL, 38372526

Our aircraft left formation near Frankfurt, Germany. Part of the crew bailed out. 2nd Lt. Dink, T/Sgt. Williams and myself bailed out near Frankfurt. 2nd Lt. Filer, 2nd Lt. La Vigna and T/Sgt. Mochetti were in the cockpit when our ship struck the ground. S/Sgt. Beck and S/Sgt. Brogen were dead in the waist. No knowledge on others.

S/Sgt. Fred R. Beck, 34605802, did not bail out. He was dead lying in waist of our ship.
T/Sgt. Lido R. Mochetti, 31214993, did not bail out.
S/Sgt. Carl E. Brogren Jr., 18214993, did not bail out. He was dead lying in waist of our ship.
2nd Lt. Fred K. LaVigna, 0814918, did not bail out. He was lying over on the controls.
2nd Lt. Charles W. Filer, 0810854, did not bail out.

12 MAY 1944, 8TH AF, 96TH BG, 338TH BS

Target: Brux (Most), Czechoslovakia
Aircraft type, model and series: B-17G, Serial No. 42-31343
Engines - type, model and series: R-1820-97
Engine Nos. (a) SW-002576 (b) 43-60753 (c) 43-64179 (d) 41-24094
Nickname of aircraft: Unknown
Type of mission: Bombing
aircraft was lost as a result of enemy aircraft. Aircraft last seen at 1210 hours approximately at 50/10 N, 07/10 E.
Point of departure: AAF STA 138

CREW POSITION, NAME IN FULL

Lewis, Robert W.	1st Lt, Pilot	0-810906	KIA
Soderlund, Gustaf J.	2nd Lt, Copilot	0-818065	KIA
Korty, George J., Jr.	2nd Lt, Nav.	0-702933	KIA
Foote, Kenneth W.	2nd Lt, Bomb.	0-757710	KIA
Duff, Carl T.	T/Sgt, Eng.	34722378	KIA
Herrin, Dyton W.	T/Sgt, RORG	19202957	KIA
Klecha, Alexander J.	S/Sgt, Asst. Eng. RW	32460338	POW
Howard, Paul B.	S/Sgt, Asst. ROBT	34446697	POW

Corley, Forest C.	S/Sgt, TG	39125909	POW
Elliott, Kenneth E.	S/Sgt, LW	36596926	POW

REPORT ON SHOT-DOWN AMERICAN AIRCRAFT

Date and time aircraft was shot-down: 12 May 1944 at 1230 hours
Place of crash: Mershausen, Germany
Type of aircraft: B-17 Fortress
One unknown dead: could not be identified, probably 20-22 years old, slender, dark brown hair.

12 MAY 1944, 8TH AF, 100TH BG, 349TH BS

Target: Brux (Most), Czechoslovakia
Aircraft type, model and series: B-17G, Serial No. 42-97127
Engines - type, model and series: R-1820-97
Engine Nos. (a) SW-007140 (b) SW-005637 (c) 43-61065 (d) SW-005739
Nickname of aircraft: Unknown
Type of mission: Bombing
Aircraft was lost as a result of antiaircraft fire.
Point of departure: AAF STA 139

CREW POSITION, NAME IN FULL

Moore, Jack C.	1st Lt, Pilot	0-745143	POW
Blais, Robert L.	2nd Lt, Copilot	0-755853	POW
McClure, Ross O.	F/O, Nav.	T-123149	POW
Whidby, Monroe T.	2nd Lt, Bomb.	0-689510	POW
Kidner, John P.	T/Sgt, RO	15394576	POW
Heiber, Henry	T/Sgt, Eng.	33414300	POW
Dishneau, Wilbur G.	S/Sgt, BTG	16149221	KIA
Jedryck, John J.	S/Sgt, RWG	6997362	POW
Hunter, James R.	S/Sgt, LWG	17090397	POW
Mueller, Charles R.	S/Sgt, TG	6831088	POW

REPORT ON CAPTURED AIRCRAFT

Date and time aircraft was shot-down: 12 May 1944 about 1400 hours.

Place of crash: north side of Georgendorf, 20 km northwest of Bruex (Sudeten) 30 km southeast of Freiberg

Kind of capture: probably anti-aircraft

Type of aircraft: Fortress B-17G 40

Markings of aircraft: R*I

Equipment: Camera, Aircraft, 5x7 inch Type K21

Condition of aircraft: According to the location of the main parts of the aircraft it is supposed, that the engines fall first. One propeller, still undamaged at the engine, stands in feathered position. The engine in question therefore must have been fallen at first.

The fuselage has loosened from the wing and has broken into two parts.

The nose turret and the tail end are lying pressed flat about 15 meters apart. All installations are destroyed and lie scattered on the field. The wing inner section is destroyed by fire caused by crash. The wing tips lie about one kilometer apart.

Crew: Presumably nine. One dead buried at Georgendorf, Sudeten. Presumably one at hospital in Bruex. Presumably four in Saxony or Sudeten, disposition unknown. Gestapo has already inquired.

12 MAY 1944, 8TH AF, 96TH BG, 337TH BS

Target: Brux (Most), Czechoslovakia
Aircraft type, model and series: B-17G, Serial No. 43-64768
Engines - type, model and series: R-1820-97
Engine Nos. (a) 42-79169 (b) 43-63631 (c) 42-138268 (d) 43-64768
Nickname of aircraft: Unknown
Type of mission: Bombing
Aircraft was lost as a result of enemy aircraft (left wing destroyed and went down out of control).
Aircraft last known position: 50/10 N, 07/10 E
Point of departure: AAF STA 138

CREW POSITION, NAME IN FULL

Kinman, Wilford N.	2nd Lt, Pilot	0-801284	POW
Felty, Warren Z.	2nd Lt, Copilot	0-815866	POW
Reid, David W.	2nd Lt, Nav.	0-698084	POW
Montgomery, William C.	2nd Lt, Bomb.	0-550114	POW
Hubbard, Irwin G. Jr.	T/Sgt, Eng.	18218713	POW
Chandler, Milton E.	T/Sgt, RO	31222341	POW
Lee, Charles J.	S/Sgt, RWG	34505131	POW
Olds, Walter J.	S/Sgt, BTG	33603036	POW
Nonneman, Ernest F.	S/Sgt, LWG	37667374	POW
Ward, Rufus A.	S/Sgt, TG	13075075	POW

Date and time aircraft was shot-down: 12 May 1944 between 1230-1300
Target: Brux (Most)
Place of crash: near Friedberg

12 MAY 1944, 8TH AF, 357TH FG, 362ND FS

Target: Brux, Czechoslovakia
Aircraft type, model and series: P51B, Serial No. 43-6634
Engine - type, model and series: V-1650-5, Serial No. V-300779
Nickname of aircraft: Unknown
Aircraft last known position at 1245 hours, 23 miles north of Wurzburg, Czechoslovakia. Aircraft was lost as a result of enemy aircraft.
Place of departure: AAF St. F-373

CREW POSITION, NAME IN FULL

Roger A. Hilstad, Pilot, 2nd Lt., 0-694153, interred in private cemetery in Minnesota.

STATEMENT BY CAPT. MAURICE F. BAKER, 0-730333

I was the last person to see 2nd Lt. Roger A. Hilstad, 362nd FS, 357th FG. I last saw him about 23 miles north of Wurzburg, Czechoslovakia at 1245 hours on 12 May 1944.

I was leading Dollar Squadron when, just after rendezvous, the front box of bombers was hit by ME-109s. Lt. Hilstad, my wing man and I went down after a formation of four of them. He was right behind me on my wing during the ensuing fight on the deck. I saw a ME-109 shoot at him, but he rolled out of the way when I called for him to break. Apparently, he had not been hit. Then I went after the ME-109 which had shot

Pyote AAB, TX, 1943. Standing l-r: T/Sgt. Robert W. Mazzacane, T/Sgt. Charles J. Wilson, S/Sgt. Charles R. Daniels, S/Sgt. Eugene W. Wayrynen, S/Sgt. Charles R. Stewart. Kneeling l-r: S/Sgt. David F. Casties, 2nd Lt. Theodore R. Schmuck, 2nd Lt. Dale R. Wynn, 2nd Lt. William J. Dodd, 1st Lt. Alexander W. Kinder

at my wing man and knocked him down. After this I looked around and didn't see Lt. Hilstad. I flew around, trying to find him and contact him by radio with no results.

12 MAY 1944, 8TH AF, 100TH BG, 418TH BS

Target: Brux (Most), Czechoslovakia
Aircraft type, model and series: B-17G, Serial No. 42-31504
Engines - type, model and series: R-1820-97
Engine Nos. (a) SW-004612 (b) SW-004242 (c) 43-56753 (d) SW-004612
Nickname of aircraft: Unknown
Type of mission: Bombing
Aircraft was lost as a result of enemy anti-aircraft fire. Last seen at 1623 hours near French Coast approximately 51/07 N, 02/40 E.
Point of departure: AAF STA 139

CREW POSITION, NAME IN FULL

Kinder, Alexander W.	1st Lt, Pilot	0-754517	POW
Schmuck, Theodore R.	2nd Lt, Copilot	0-441002	POW
Wynn, Dale R.	2nd Lt, Nav.	0-814479	POW

Dodd, William J.	2nd Lt, Bomb.	0-685109	POW
Mazzacane, Robert W.	T/Sgt, RO	11103213	POW
Wilson, Charles J.	T/Sgt, Eng.	19085376	POW
Daniels, Charles R.	S/Sgt, BTG	35656757	POW
Wayrynen, Eugene W.	S/Sgt, RWG	37322324	POW
Casties, David F.	S/Sgt, LWG	14178316	POW
Stewart, Charles R.	S/Sgt, TG	18131692	POW

REPORT ON SHOT-DOWN AMERICAN AIRCRAFT

Date and time aircraft was shot-down: On 12 May 1944 at 1530 hours a four engine American bomber crashed on the South exit of the township Niederbachheim, District of St. Goarshausen. The bomber exploded and was completely destroyed.

Disposition of crew: The crew bailed out before the crash. The crew was captured by the police and civilians. POW enemy airmen were sent to Armed Forces Land Guard Batl. 786 in St. Goarshausen and from there on 15 May 1944 at 0940 hours sent to Dulag Luft Oberursel.

12 MAY 1944, 8TH AF, 96TH BG, 339TH BS

Target: Brux (Most), Czechoslovakia
Aircraft type, model and series: B-17G, Serial No. 42-107123
Engines, This was a new A/C and the numbers of the engines and the guns had not been taken off for the records.
Nickname of aircraft: Unknown
Type of mission: Bombing
Aircraft last sighted at 1210 hours at 50/10 N, 07/10 E. Aircraft was lost as a result of enemy aircraft.
Point of departure: AAF STA 138

CREW POSITION, NAME IN FULL

Tucker, Harold H.	2nd Lt, Pilot	0-869895	KIA
Greenwood, Robert A.	2nd Lt, Copilot	0-818664	KIA
Slemenski, Walter	2nd Lt, Bomb.	0-757929	KIA
Detwiler, Samuel R., Jr.	2nd Lt, Nav.	0-709308	KIA
Stoller, Lloyd D.	S/Sgt, Eng. TTG	35545015	POW
Davis, James A. Jr.	T/Sgt, RO	32440208	POW
Witt, Lawrence L.	T/Sgt, Asst. Eng. RWG	16160308	POW
Boatright, Willis D.	S/Sgt, Asst. RO BTG	34071991	POW
Maisak, Robert L.	S/Sgt, LWG	19011806	POW
Greuter, Jennings C.	S/Sgt, TG	35545269	KIA

STATEMENT BY T/SGT JAMES A. DAVIS JR. 32440208

Our aircraft left formation near Limburg, Germany. All members of crew went out the waist door; six men. Copilot 2nd Lt. Robert A. Greenwood had no chute and attempted to bail out with me, losing his grip when the chute opened.

2ND LT. ROBERT A. GREENWOOD, 0-818664

2nd Lt. Greenwood attempted to bail out when his chute was apparently burned. He came back into the radio room looking and asking for an extra chute. All he had on was a bunny heated suit and looked a bit burned. After he bailed out with me, he lost his hold on my leg and fell to the ground. After I was captured the same night at Dulag Luft, a German officer inquired if anyone belonged to Lt. Greenwood, but due to regulations, I remained silent.

12 May 1944, 8th AF, 94th BG, 331st BS

Target: Brux (Most), Czechoslovakia
Aircraft type, model and series: B-17G, Serial No. 42-31704
Engines - type, model and series: R-1820-97
Engine Nos. (a) 43-57102 (b) SW-011602 (c) SW-007448 (d) SW-009272
Nickname of aircraft: Unknown
Type of mission: Bombing
Aircraft was lost as a result of enemy aircraft. Last seen at 1238 hours at 50/25 N, 09/00 E.
Point of departure: AAF STA 468

CREW POSITION, NAME IN FULL

Walker, Walter L.	2nd Lt, Pilot	0-808483	POW
Brice, George H.	1st Lt, Copilot	0-748545	POW
Salotti, Aldo R.	2nd Lt, Nav.	0-703805	POW
Gibler, Clinton W.	2nd Lt, Bomb.	0-756870	KIA
Blais, Joseph C.	S/Sgt, RO	31278854	POW
Smith, William A.	Sgt, BTG	17061828	POW
Hayes, Payton T., Jr.	S/Sgt, TTG,	34503522	POW
Letvin, Michael	Sgt, RWG	15323215	KIA
Stasko, Paul J.	Sgt, LWG	35335916	POW
Williams, Charles N.	Sgt, TG	19137721	POW

REPORT ON SHOT-DOWN AMERICAN AIRCRAFT

Date and time aircraft was shot-down: 12 May 1944 at 1240 hours
Place of crash: The four engine aircraft is lying 300 m east of Hofgut Altenburg Farm, Community of Bad Orb. Rail road station Bad Orb.
Kind of capture: Shot-down by day fighter
Type of aircraft: B-17, Fortress
Condition of aircraft: Aircraft completely damaged by explosion of the bombs. Wreckage spread over 500 m. Nacelle and engine destruction 99%. Parts of five MG was found.

12 May 1944, 8th AF, 452nd BG, 729th BS

Target: Brux (Most), Czechoslovakia
Aircraft type, model and series: B-17G, Serial No. 42-97143
Engines - type, model and series: R-1820-97
Engines Nos. (a) SW-072901 (b) SW-007204 (c) SW-007255 (c) SW-007699
Nickname of aircraft: Unknown
Type of mission: Bombing
Aircraft last seen at 1215 hours approximately at 50/17 N, 07/40 E. Aircraft lost as a result of enemy aircraft.
Point of departure: AAA STA 142

CREW POSITION, NAME IN FULL

Stogsdill, Otis L.	2nd Lt, Pilot	0-687779	RTD
Daniels, Joseph D.	2nd Lt, Copilot	0-753984	KIA
O'Brien, William H.	2nd Lt, Nav.	0-692332	KIA
Gricoo, Louis J.	2nd Lt, Bomb.	0-688526	KIA
Dean, Ernest C.	T/Sgt, TTG	15118377	RTD

2nd Lt. Marshall V. Peterson, 0-693312, remains not recovered, memorialized at Florence American Military Cemetery, Florence, Italy

The Ardennes American Military Cemetery, Neuville-en-Condroz, Belgium

The Ardennes American Military Cemetery, Neuville-en-Condroz, Belgium.

2nd Lt. Frank P. Marcus, 0-1703140

S/Sgt. A.W. Lain, 18187319

2nd Lt. Charles H. McNally, 0-694573

T/Sgt. George G. Hadfield, 17154453

S/Sgt. Charles C. Gibson, 35508784

Weber, Karl A.	T/Sgt, RO	32739060	KIA
Williams, Robert E.	S/Sgt, BTG	35092504	KIA
Andrews, Frank A.	S/Sgt, RWG	32552582	KIA
Walsh, Michael J.	S/Sgt, LWG	32806101	KIA
Redmond, James C.	S/Sgt, TG	18231815	KIA

16 JUN 1944, 15TH AF, 376TH BG, 515TH BS

Target: Bratislava, Czechoslovakia
Aircraft type, model and series: B-24G, Serial No. 42-78209
Engines - type, model and series: R-1830-65
Engine Nos. (a) BP-426472 (b) BP-426505 (c) BP-426592 (d) BP-426596
Nickname of aircraft: Unknown
Type of mission: High altitude bombing. Aircraft was lost as a result of enemy aircraft. Last sighted at 47/57 N, 18/03 E.
Point of departure: San Pancrazio, Italy

CREW POSITION, NAME IN FULL

Marcus, Frank P.	2nd Lt, Pilot	0-1703140	Massillon, OH	KIA
Peterson, Marshall V.	2nd Lt, Copilot	0-693312	Watertown, S	KIA
McNally, Charles H.	2nd Lt, Nav.	0-694573	Annapolis, MD	KIA
Schoenlein, Donald L.	2nd Lt, Bomb	0-690829	Portland, IN	POW
Hadfield, George G.	T/Sgt, Eng.	17154453	Minneapolis, MN	KIA
Fahr, William F.	T/Sgt, RO	32658590	Melville, NY	KIA
Gibson, Charles C.	S/Sgt, Gunner	35508784	Evansville, IN	KIA
Keyes, George R.	S/Sgt, Gunner	32737559	Elmira, NY	KIA
Lain, A.W.	S/Sgt, Gunner	18187319	Frankston, TX	KIA
Wiles, Carleton E.	S/Sgt, Gunner	33459822	New Albany, PA	KIA

Statement By Sgt. Kenneth Jackson, 19082352.

I saw ME-210 blow up right under the trailing edge of aircraft No. 42-78209, The right wing of No. 42-78209 then came off and exploded. Ship then went down in a spin.

Statement By S/Sgt. Elmer R. Burkhardt, 33578555

I was flying about hundred yards from aircraft No. 42-78209 when enemy aircraft knocked the right wing of No. 42-78209 off. One chute was seen to open from aircraft.

Report On Shot-Down Aircraft

Date and time aircraft was shot-down: 16 Jun 1944
Place of crash: Komarno, Czechoslovakia
Type of aircraft: Liberator
2nd Lt. Donald L. Schoenlein, 0-690892, captured, Dulag Luft III
2nd Lt. Frank P. Marcus 0-1703140
2nd Lt. Charles H. McNally 0-694573
T/Sgt. George G. Hadfield 17134453
S/Sgt. Charles C. Gibson 35508784
S/Sgt. A.W. Lain 18187319, Ardennes American Military Cemetery, Neuville-en-Condroz, Belgium
2nd Lt. Marshall V. Peterson 0-693312, remains not recovered
T/Sgt. William F. Fahr, 32658590, Long Island National Cemetery, Farmingdale, NY
S/Sgt. George R. Keyes, 32737559, Woodlawn National Cemetery, Elmira, NY
S/Sgt. Carleton E. Wiles, 33459822, Private Cemetery, New Albany, PA

16 Jun 1944, 15th AF, 450th BG, 723rd BS

Target: Bratislava (Apollo Oil Refinery), Czechoslovakia
Aircraft type, model and series: B-24G, Serial No. 42-78104
Engines - type, model and series: P&W R-1830
Engine Nos. (a) 42-58899 (b) 42-58714 (c) CP-305203 (d) 42-58728
Nickname of aircraft: Unknown
Type of mission: Bombing
Aircraft was lost as a result of enemy aircraft and was seen to crash.
Last sighted at 47/32 N, 17/00 E
Point of departure: Manduria, Italy

Crew position, name in full

Koegel, Peter C.	2nd Lt, Pilot	0-818166	Bayside, NY	POW
Kane, John E.	2nd Lt, Copilot	0-822990	Brooklyn, NY	POW
Collins, Joseph G.	2nd Lt, Nav.	0-709294	Boston, MA	POW
Yancey, Wallace D.	2nd Lt, Bomb	0-708990	Fort Worth, TX	POW
Kampstra, Renard G.	S/Sgt, Eng.	16143998	Chicago, IL	POW
Harris, Melvin	Sgt, RO	31370499	Brookline, MA	KIA
Malawsky, Irving B.	S/Sgt, Gunner	36738921	Chicago, IL	POW
McClintock, Charles H.	Sgt, Gunner	33429907	West Newton, P	POW
Klock, Floyd K.	Sgt, NG	32942549	Ogdensburg, NY	KIA
Hall, Louis C.	S/Sgt, AAG	37283442	Little Falls, MN	POW

Statement By S/Sgt. Leon M. Claverie, 39035056

On 16 Jun 1944 our group was on a mission to bomb the target at Bratislava, Czechoslovakia. I was flying as ball gunner in the lead ship in the low left element of the second attack unit; 2nd Lt. Koegel's ship number 42-78104 was in the same element. On the return route from the target our formation was attacked by enemy fighters, Six of the fighters attacked 2nd Lt. Koegel's ship. The ship was apparently hit since it lost altitude and left formation. Soon afterwards three men bailed out; however, one chute failed to open. The ship made a turn and six men bailed out at regular intervals. The ship then made another turn and the last man bailed out. The ship went into a dive and blew upon hitting the ground. The time was 0825 hours and the coordinates were 47/32 N, 17/00 E.

Sgt. Melvin Harris, 31370499, and Sgt. Floyd K. Klock, 32942549, are interred at Long Island National Cemetery, Farmingdale, NY.

26 Jun 1944, 15th AF, 82nd FG, 95th FS

Target: Vienna-Austria
Aircraft type, model and series: P-38J 15LO, Serial No. 43-28771
Engine - type, model and series: (L) A-045659, (R) A-045318, V-1710-91, V-1710-89
Nickname of aircraft: Unknown
Type of mission: Bomber escort
Aircraft last known position: 30 miles ESE of Vienna, Austria at 0920. Aircraft P-38J was lost as a result of enemy aircraft and seen to crash.
Place of departure: Vincenzo No. 11, Italy.

Crew position, name in full

Wisner, Jacob Allen   2nd Lt, Pilot   0-760216   Grand Rapids, MI   POW

26 Jun 1944, 15th AF, 82nd FG, 95th FS

Target: Vienna-Austria
Aircraft type, model and series: P-38J 15LO, Serial No. 42-104393
Engine - type, model and series: (L) A-038766 (R) A-036202, V-1710-91, V-1710-89
Nickname of aircraft: Unknown
Type of mission: Bomber escort
Aircraft last known position: 30 miles ESE of Vienna, Austria at 0930. Aircraft P-38J was lost probably as a result of mechanical trouble. Place of departure: Vincenzo No. 11, Italy.

Crew position, name in full

*Allen, Wallace Ray   2nd Lt, Pilot   0-754455   Girard, IL   KIA

*On 3/4 Sep 1990 remains of pilot recovered near Bratislava (JUR), Czechoslovakia and repatriated to USA

26 Jun 1944, 15th AF, 461st BG, 766th BS

Target: Korneuburg, Austria
Aircraft type, model and series: B-24H, Serial No. 41-28679
Engines - type, model and series: R-1830-43
Engine Nos. (a) 42-91365 (b) 42-62384 (c) 42-85847 (d) 42-62471
Nickname of aircraft: *Heaven Can Wait*
Type of mission: Bombing

T/Sgt. Albert F. Carlock, 39455785

Aircraft was lost as a result of other circumstances, aborted and failed to return to home base.
Point of departure: Torretta, Italy

CREW POSITION, NAME IN FULL

Zive, Samuel M.	2nd Lt, Pilot	0-1683594	Los Angeles, CA	POW
Mailhot, Bertrand R.	F/O, Copilot	T-123185	Pawtucket, RI	POW
Schonzeit, Marvin	2nd Lt, Bomb.	0-668790	Brooklyn, NY	POW
Laulis, James C.	2nd Lt, Nav.	0-692029	Shinnston, WV	POW
Carlock, Albert F.	T/Sgt, RWG	39455785	Wenatchee, WA	KIA
Schwartz, Murray	S/Sgt, TG	12191951	Brooklyn, NY	POW
Thomas, Perry J.	T/Sgt, BTG	18194676	Sharon, OK	KIA
Clark, Bevins	S/Sgt, NG	15108354	Fort Wayne, IN	P0W
Turner, Robert M.	Sgt, TG	32378584	Oswego, NY	KIA
Wiemann, Ned W.	S/Sgt, LWG	37553636	Arlington, MN	POW

STATEMENT BY S/SGT. BEVINS CLARK, 15108354

Our aircraft left formation over Czechoslovakia - visible was flak area of Wiener Neustadt.
Pilot 2nd Lt. Zive, Bomb. 2nd Lt. Schonzeit and S/Sgt. Schwartz (wounded) bailed out from bomb bay. S/Sgt. Wiemann

T/Sgt. Perry J. Thomas 18194676

out waist window and Nav. 2nd Lt. Laulis out nose wheel well. Other three: T/Sgt. Thomas, Sgt. Turner and T/Sgt. Carlock, did not leave aircraft. All three burned to death.

T/Sgt. Albert F. Carlock, 39455785

T/Sgt. Carlock did not bail out. He was wounded in leg but able to move around. He was last seen in waist ready to leave aircraft but reason for not leaving is unknown.

T/Sgt. Perry J, Thomas, 18194676

T/Sgt. Thomas did not bail out. Last seen standing in waist ready to leave aircraft out waist and there is no known reason why he didn't follow S/Sgt. Wiemann out.

Sgt. Robert M. Turner, 32378584

Sgt. Turner did not bail out. Sgt. Turner was seriously wounded. He had been hit in stomach by 20mm and was unable to leave aircraft.

T/Sgt. Albert F. Carlock, 39455785, and T/Sgt. Perry J. Thomas, 18194676, are interred at Lorraine American Military Cemetery, St. Avold, France. Sgt. Robert M. Turner, 32378584 is interred in a private cemetery in Oswego, NY.

26 Jun 1944, 15th AF, 459th BG, 758th BS

Target: Oil Refinery 25 miles west of Vienna, Austria
Aircraft type, model and series: B-24H, Serial No. 41-28674
Engines - type, model and series: R-183043
Engine Nos. (a) 41-43589 (b) 42-62296 (c) 42-62379 (d) 42-9271
Nickname of aircraft: Unknown
Type of mission: Bombing
Aircraft last sighted at 1020 hours near Vep, Austria. No apparent reason for disappearance of aircraft.
Point of departure: Giuilia, Italy

CREW POSITION, NAME IN FULL

Artz, Lincoln E.	2nd Lt Pilot	0-697328	Rochester, NY	POW
Lowe, Bruce L.	2nd Lt, Copilot	0-822035	Flint, MI	POW
Ryan, Leo A.	2nd Lt, Bomb.	0-678469	New Brunswick, NJ	POW
Fuquay, Frank J.	S/Sgt, Eng.	35727866	Evansville, IN	POW
Zambo, George C.	S/Sgt, RO	36814701	Cudahy, WI	POW
Johnson, Bryce K.	Sgt, Gunner	37558155	Bowman, ND	POW
Donatelli, Edward E.	Sgt, Gunner	33283544	Pittsburgh, PA	POW
Moulton, Richard W.	Sgt, Gunner	11139177	Melrose, MA	POW
Shea, Edward J.	Sgt, Gunner	42004278	Jersey City, NJ	POW

Crew of 2nd Lt. L.E. Artz. Standing l-r: Nav. Lindsey (not on mission), 2nd Lt. Lincoln E. Artz, 2nd Lt. Leo A. Ryan, Copilot 2nd Lt. Dave Goldberg (not on mission). Kneeling l-r: Sgt. Edward J. Shea, S/Sgt. Frank J. Fuquay, Sgt. Richard W. Moulton, S/Sgt.George C. Zambo. Sitting l-r: Sgt. Edward E. Donatelli, Sgt. Bryce K. Johnson

*P-51D, WD * R Serial No. 44-13487 landed near Vracov District of Hodonin, Czechoslovakia (36 km SW from Uherske Hradiste).*

ESCAPE STATEMENT

Sgt. Edward E. Donatelli, 33283544, 459th BG, 758th BS, born 26 Jan 1920, enlisted 14 Jul 1942, MIA 26 Jun 1944. Interrogated 8 Oct 1944. Duty: Tail Gunner

S/Sgt. Frank J. Fuquay, 35727866, 459th BG, 758th BS, born 25 Oct 1924, enlisted 20 Mar 1943, MIA 26 Jun 1944. Interrogated 8 Oct 1944. Duty: Engineer.

On way to Vienna, Austria we had trouble with number one and number three run away props and had to feather number two. Number four engine was losing manifold pressure. Left formation five minutes before target time. Pilot 2nd Lt. Lincoln E. Artz, 0-697328, notified crew to bail out. Bailed out and landed on border between Hungary and Slovakia. Landed at town of Miloslava. After landing was captured by Hungarians. They took all clothes shoes and socks and made the prisoners walk barefooted. Since they were captured in Slovakia by Hungarians, the Slovaks took the prisoners away from the Hungarians. The Hungarians kept all of the personal possessions of the Americans. The Slovakians treated the prisoners well. Went from Miloslava to Bratislava, then taken to military hospital where they stayed two weeks.

On 8 Aug 1944 went to military barracks at Bratislava where they stayed until 12 Aug 1944 when they left for Grenova. When Germans started taking over Slovakia the prisoners were released by prison officials. After leaving prison camp on 2 Sep 1944, the first village was Pezinok then to Modra, to Trnava and to a small town 10 miles south of Piestany. There met two Partisans who fed them and let them sleep in their barn. Later went to Cicmany, Rajec and to town Banska Bystrica. All evacuated from the Tri Duby A/D North from Banska Bystrica.

30 Jun 1944, 15th AF, 52nd FG, 4th FS

Target: Blechhammer, Poland
Aircraft type, model and series: P-51D 5NA, Sqn. Ltrs. WD-R
Serial No. 44-13487
Engine - type, model and series: V-1650-7, Serial No. V-322189
Nickname of aircraft: Unknown
Type of mission: Bomber escort
Aircraft last known position: 49.48N/18.35E near Trencin, Czechoslovakia
Aircraft P-51D was lost as pilot bellied in enemy territory.
Place of departure: Madna, Italy

CREW POSITION, NAME IN FULL

Kurtz, Max Merle	2nd Lt, Pilot	0-766369	Nyssa, OR	POW

On 30 Jun 1944 the 52nd FG, 4th FS was flying Bomber Escort mission to Blechhammer, Poland - 2nd, 4th, 5th Squadron participating.

Mission and target: To provide cover over target and on withdrawal for the 5th, 49th and 304th Wings of the 15th AF, attacking Blechhammer, Poland synthetic oil plants at 1030-100 hours. Probably because of weather no bombers were seen.

49 P-51s took off from Madna A/D at 0815 hours; 14 aircraft returned early—eight mechanical, one pilot, five escort; one aircraft was lost; 34 aircraft landed at Madna A/D at 1310 hours.

4th Squadron: At about 1100 hours Lt. Kurtz was seen by Lt. Hanes to belly land at 49-48N, 18-35E. No reason was apparent and there was no report on R/T. Lt. Kurtz was last seen standing beside his aircraft apparently unhurt

52nd FG, 4th FS P-51D, WD*R, Ser. No. 44-13487. Piloted by 2nd Lt. Max Merle Kurtz, 0-766369, bellied in enemy territory near Vracov, district of Hodonin, Czechoslovakia. Pilot captured.

STATEMENT BY 2ND LT. WILLIAM F. HANES JR.

Lt. Kurtz, 0-766369, was flying my wing in Blue section of the 4th Squadron at 26,000 feet. When at about 1100 hours, without an R/T call or a signal of any kind, he suddenly dropped back in formation. I made a 180 degree turn to go back to him and he was heading down in a glide, on course. I circled him all the way down, through overcast and clear with still no sign of distress from Lt. Kurtz.

Lt. M.M. Kurtz bellied his aircraft in a field at 49-48N, 18-35E on what appeared to be a roadway. I circled and buzzed him to try and see what had happened to him, and noticed him standing beside his aircraft, apparently unhurt, but no attempt to leave the aircraft and some people were walking up the road toward him. Not wishing to remain on the deck alone any longer, I climbed back to above an overcast at 20,000 feet and bellow another at 24,000 feet and came home.

7 JUL 1944, 15TH AF, 463RD BG, 773RD BS

Target: Blechhammer, Poland
Aircraft type, model and series: B-17G, Serial No. 42-31775
Engines - type, model and series: (a) SW-00657 (b) SW-006563 (c) SW-006623 (d) SW-008781
Nickname of aircraft: *Easy 5*
Type of mission: Bombing
Aircraft was lost as a result of enemy aircraft. Aircraft last seen at 0948 hours 47/16 N, 17/58 E
Point of departure: Celone, Italy

CREW POSITION, NAME IN FULL

Sorenson, Carl C., Jr.	2nd Lt, Pilot	0-755775	Wabasha, MN	KIA
Enoch, Kingsley B.	2nd Lt, Copilot	0-819676	Springfield, MA	KIA
Berrie, Albert L.	2nd Lt, Nav.	0-690350	Belmont, MA	KIA
Platten, Thomas V.	1st Lt, Bomb.	0-667346	Modesto, CA	KIA
Sharp, Kenneth E.	T/Sgt, TTG	18209411	Campti, LA	KIA
Delio, Danny	S/Sgt, RWG	36581669	Mishawaka, IN	KIA
Rossi, Ernest R.	S/Sgt, LWG	19139628	Oakland, CA	KIA
Kennelley, Harold R.	T/Sgt, RO	33567818	Spring Mills, PA	KIA
Nye, Donald L.	S/Sgt, BTG	35344537	Tiffin, OH	KIA
Leone, John R.	S/Sgt, TG	12821957	Bronx, NY	KIA

Date and time aircraft was shot-down: 7 Jul 1944 at 1000 hours.
Target: Blechhammer, Poland
Type of aircraft: Fortress
Place of crash: Calovo, Slovakia
Crew: 10 dead

7 JUL 1944, 15TH AF, 463RD BG, 774TH BS

Target: Blechhammer, Poland
Aircraft type, model and series: B-17G, Serial No. 42-102889
Engines - type, model and series: R-1820-97
Engine Nos. (a) 43-145714 (b) 43-145601 (c) SW-011574 (d) 43-145680
Nickname of aircraft: Unknown
Type of mission: Bombing
Aircraft was lost as a result of enemy anti-aircraft fire. Last seen at approximately 1010 hours, 50/20 N, 18/15 E.
Point of departure: Celone, Italy
Date and time aircraft was shot-down: 7 Jul 1944 at 1100 hours
Target: Blechhammer, Poland
Type of aircraft: Fortress
Place of crash: Uherske Hradiste, Moravia

CREW POSITION, NAME IN FULL

Lindbloom, Edward M.	2nd Lt, Pilot	0-753225	Wood, SD	POW
Sant, John M.	1st Lt, Copilot	0-815245	Pittsburgh, PA	POW
Beatty, John S.	2nd Lt, Nav.	0-694532	Cincinnati, OH	POW
Edgar, Raymond O.	2nd Lt, Bomb.	0-762087	Dunn Station, PA	POW
Cruca, Harold L.	T/Sgt, UT	35423852	Muncie, IN	POW
Shinnick, Lawrence W.	T/Sgt, RG	13076207	Frederick, MD	POW
Duncan, Colonel L.	S/Sgt, BT	38465211	Tulsa, OK	POW
Allen, William J.	S/Sgt, LW	33599768	Philadelphia, PA	POW
Roberts, William E., Jr.	S/Sgt, RW	13107432	McKeesport, PA	POW
Mack, William J.	S/Sgt, TG	16098139	Richmond, VA	KIA

William J. Mack was buried 8 Jul 1944 in cemetery Velehrad, Row 2, Grave 3, southwest side.
S/Sgt William J. Mack, 16098139, buried in a private cemetery in Illinois.

7 JUL 1944, 15TH AF, 2ND BG, 96TH BS

Target: Blechhammer, Poland
Aircraft type, model and series: B-17G, Serial No. 42-97183
Engines - type, model and series: R-1820-97
Engine Nos. (a) SW-011125 (b) SW-013890 (c) 42-138545 (d) SW-008041
Nickname of aircraft: Unknown
Type of mission: Bombing
Aircraft was lost as a result of engine trouble then turned back and was attacked by three ME-109s. Last seen at 1028 hours 49/30 N,   17/25 E,
Point of departure: Amendola, Italy

CREW POSITION, NAME IN FULL

Corpening, Ira B.	1st Lt, Pilot	0-755284	Salinas, CA	POW
Kellogg, John F.	2nd Lt, Copilot	0-751345	Santa Monica, CA	POW
De Voe, William D.	2nd Lt, Nav.	0-749819	Roswell, NM	POW
Gallup, Robert F.	2nd Lt, Bomb.	0-739423	Crumlynne, PA	POW
Skinner, Norton D.	T/Sgt, UTG	16169858	Chicago, IL	POW
Stultz, Shields G.	S/Sgt, LTG	13120896	Ridgeway, VA	POW
Brau, Paul J.	S/Sgt, RWG	37033438	Atkinson, NE	POW
Leszezynski, William J.	S/Sgt, LWG	11113656	Wooster, MA	POW
Strode, Samuel L., Jr.	S/Sgt, LWG	17159203	New London, MO	POW
Stuart, Virgil R.	T/Sgt, ROG	37501688	Carthage, MO	POW

ESCAPE STATEMENT OF NORTON D. SKINNER

T/Sgt. Norton D. Skinner, 16169858, 2nd BG, 96th BS, born 24 Feb 1924, enlisted 10 Dec 1942, MIA 7 Jul 1944, interrogated 8 Oct 1944, duty: engineer-gunner.

Over Slovakia on way to target some stray bullets from enemy fighters hit number four engine. Engine seemed okay, but soon noticed number one cylinder head protruding through ring column. Couldn't feather. Couldn't hold position. Salvoed bombs and aircraft turned back. Ring cowling flew off, cut big gash in wing and hung there. Terrific vibration.

In view of situation with enemy fighters, crew decided to leave ship. All out okay. T/Sgt. Skinner saw ship crash, then he was hidden by peasants. T/Sgt. Skinner believes that several others of crew were taken by Germans who were searching area. He stayed under cover for awhile then contacted peasants again and was given food and water. After he was left Slovak Gendarmes picked him up. He was searched and remained over night at their station. Next day to Bratislava and from there to Grenava Prison Camp. Later on 19 Sep 1944 on way to evacuation point at Tri Duby airfield near Banska

Bystrica, Slovakia. T/Sgt. Skinner left Czechoslovakia with following American airmen: T/Sgt. Claude Henry Davis, 2nd Lt. George O. Winberg, 2nd Lt. Neal T. Cobb, S/Sgt. Jesse Houston, 2nd Lt. Frank C. Soltesz and a few others he can't recall.

Escape Statement of Samuel L. Strode

S/Sgt. Samuel L. Strode, 17159203, 2nd BG, 96th BS, born 5 Nov 1922, enlisted 26 Oct 1942, MIA 7 Jul 1944, interrogated 18 Sep 1944, duty as tail gunner.

On 7 Jul 1944 our aircraft was attacked by enemy fighters and put out of control. S/Sgt. Strode bailed out at Senica, Slovakia at order of pilot. He landed at about 1130 hours. He hid his parachute and himself in tall weeds nearby. After hiding for short period of time, he began to travel south through the hills towards Yugoslavia.

Two days later, S/Sgt. Strode was captured by a forest ranger and was turned over to the police. He spent his first night at the police station and the next morning was taken to Trnava, remained a few hours and was then sent to Bratislava by train.

On 16 Aug 1944 transported to Grenava Prison Camp. On 2 Sep 1944 the Germans moved in and the Slovaks released POWs. A sergeant in the Scots Guard and S/Sgt. Strode traveled by foot to Rosendal, where a farmer was contacted and he took them to a Slovak officer. The Slovak officer put them in the hands of the underground who moved them to Brezova where they remained for two days. Here they met 14 other released POWs from Grenava. From here they all traveled eastward to the evacuation point at Tri Duby near Banska Bystrica.

7 Jul 1944, 15th AF, 464th BG, 778th BS

Target: Blechhammer, Poland
Aircraft type, model and series: B-24-H, Serial No. 42-52489
Engines - type, model and series: R-1830-43
Engine Nos. (a) BP-400722 (b) BP-303289 (c) 42-43748 (d) CP-303317
Nickname of aircraft: Unknown
Type of mission: Bombing
Aircraft was lost as a result of unknown cause
Aircraft last seen at approximately 1105 hours 49/15 N, 18/40 E
Point of departure: Pantanella, Italy

Crew position, name in full

Green, Earcel R.	2nd Lt, Pilot	0-813690	Cambell, MO	KIA
Gulledge, Roy L.	2nd Lt, Copilot	0-818145	Savannah, GA	KIA
Winberg, George O.	2nd Lt, Nav.	0-703355	Alameda, CA	POW/Evadee
Cobb, Neal T.	2nd Lt, Bomb.	0-699310	Whiting, IN	POW/Evadee
Davis, Claude H. Jr.	T/Sgt, Eng.	34708368	Eufaula, AL	POW/Evadee
Elliot, Jack E.	T/Sgt, RO	13119201	Richmond, VA	KIA
Howland, Gerald E.	S/Sgt, AG	37109806	Cresco, IA	POW/Evadee
Houston, Jesse C.	S/Sgt, AG	13064943	Richmond, VA	POW/Evadee
Schianca, John J.	S/Sgt, AG	31106819	Thompsonville, CT	POW/Evadee
Parker, Andrew C.	S/Sgt, AG	34776541	Wilkesboro, NC	KIA

Escape Statements

2nd Lt. George O. Winberg, 0-703355, 464th BG, 778th BS, born 15 Oct 1916, enlisted 9 Jul 1942, MIA 7 Jul 1944, interrogated 8 Oct 1944, duty as navigator.

2nd Lt. Neal T. Cobb, 0-699310, 464th BG, 778th BS, born 6 Jun 1924, enlisted 8 Jul 1942, MIA 7 Jul 1944, interrogated 8 Oct 1944, duty as bombardier.

T/Sgt. Claude H. Davis Jr., 34708368, 464th BG, 778th BS, born 10 Jan 1923, enlisted 3 Mar 1943, MIA 7 Jul 1944, interrogated 8 Oct 1944, duty as engineer.

Back Row, L-R: Unknown, Sapper Leslie Gordon John Follas, 2nd Lt. George O. Winberg, Unknown, 2nd Lt. Neal T. Cobb, Jan Repta Partisan Commander and rest unknown.

S/Sgt. Jesse C. Houston, 13064943, 464th BG, 778th BS, born 12 Mar 1924, enlisted 8 Jul 1942, MIA 7 Jul 1944, interrogated 8 Oct 1944, duty as gunner.

7 JUL 1944, BLECHHAMMER, POLAND

On 7 Jul 1944 just after bombs away 88 burst on number three engine, tail gunner S/Sgt. John James Schianca, 31106819, was hit by this burst. Our ship dropped out of formation quite rapidly. We received two or three more bursts on ship, many holes, bombsight demolished, tires blown, fuel lines, hydraulic lines cut, etc.—badly damaged.

Bomb. 2nd Lt. Neal T. Cobb, 0-699310, injured hand and leg, Navigator 2nd Lt. George O. Winberg, 0-703355, cut on hands standing on flight deck. 2nd Lt. Winberg and T/Sgt. Claude H. Davis Jr., 34708368, trying to repair leaks; waist gunner went to aid of tail gunner S/Sgt. Schianca and 2nd Lt. Cobb manned vacated waist gun.

Going down rapidly - still running on four engines at 15,000 feet - no superchargers. Feeding number four engine off number three due to leaks in number four line.

Pilot 2nd Lt. Earcel R. Green, 0-813690, tells 2nd Lt. Winberg in conversation that they better get out. 2nd Lt. Winberg got radio operator T/Sgt. Jack E. Elliott, 13119201, and nose gunner in nose and said to them get out. Opened nose door.

They asked 2nd Lt. Winberg to go out first (he did) nose gunner followed at 2,500 feet off the ground. I don't think radio operator jumped.

T/Sgt. Claude H. Davis, 34708368, took tail gunner out of turret and bandaged leg trying to make him comfortable. T/Sgt. Davis bailed out at 600 feet, chute opened at 100 feet up. Was picked up and sent to Trencin.

Slovak Lieutenant seemed willing to help get men out of camp when approached by 2nd Lt. George O. Winberg and 2nd Lt. Frank C. Soltesz, 0-697232. Were told they'd know two days before. Germans were near at this time. Planned

Sapper Leslie Gordon John Follas 30724 in center with two Slovak Partisans. Sapper Leslie Gordon John Follas 30724 was a New Zealand soldier who escaped from an Italian POW camp, Campo PG 57, and evaded to Slovakia where he was again captured and kept in POW camp near Brezova where he escaped and joined the Slovak Partisans. Sapper Follas became a fearless Partisan who was finally wounded in a shoot out with a German Patrol and was recaptured in February 1945.

finally their own escape. Slovak soldiers uneasy on day they left camp. Germans were in Bratislava, Slovakia. Everyone was told to get ready and wait. Slovak Lieutenant was to try for cars for transportation. He left for small town and said if not back in 20 minutes to leave camp. All men waited for 35 minutes and Slovak Lieutenant did not come back. Americans opened gate and all took off. We left at 1:55 a.m. on 2 Sep 1944 and Germans arrived at 2.30 a.m. T/Sgt. Claude H. Davis, S/Sgt. Jesse C. Houston, 2nd Lt. Frank C. Soltesz, 2nd Lt. Neal T. Cobb and 2nd Lt. George O. Winberg headed north and traveled steady for 15 hours. Slept in woods that night. Next day started out again. Went to Modra, got food on outskirts, continued to mountains. Met a peasant who gave them food, dried clothes and let them sleep in barn. Started next day met a peasant and he sent them into town free of Germans to a Slovak soldier. He fed, clothed them and they slept that night. Next day he pointed them in right direction. Americans went to Dobra Voda. Met a man there who took them to Brasova and Ptano. Stayed four days. Finally became a party of 15th Air Force men. Germans came in and they left. They crossed

Sapper Leslie Gordon John Follas 30724, the second man on the left with group of evading American airmen. The American airman on the left of Sapper Follas is 2nd Lt. George O. Winberg 0-703355 (B-24H, Ser. No. 42-52489). The fifth American airman is 2nd Lt. Neal T. Cobb 0-699310 (B-24H, Ser. No. 42-52489) and rest of the men unknown.

Three New Zealand Soldiers, Cairo, Egypt, 1942. L-R: Les Smith, Maurice Follas, Gordon Follas

Wreckage of P-51B, Ser. No. 43-24895 piloted by 2nd Lt. Frank C. Soltesz. Aircraft exploded in mid-air and crashed near Myjava, Slovakia.

Vah valley. Stayed with friendly people that day. Got to Zavada pod Ciernym Vrchom where stayed for two days. Joined by 11 American airmen. Slovak guide took them to St. Martin. Then to Banska Bystrica and two weeks later evacuated from Tri Duby A/D to Bari, Italy.

2nd Lt. Neal T. Cobb, 0-699310, went back to man waist gun and tail gunner S/Sgt. Schianca was brought to escape hatch—he was okay. Ball gunner S/Sgt. Andrew C. Parker, 34776541, got out of ball and manned tail gun. Engineer T/Sgt. Claude H. Davis, 34708368, was up at bomb bays working on gas leak. Pilot 2nd Lt. Earcel R. Green, 0-913690, says necessary to bail out. S/Sgt. Houston, 2nd Lt. Cobb, S/Sgt. Schianca and S/Sgt. Parker all together. Then T/Sgt. Davis came back. Told to wait at waist by pilot. Ship got very low when Pilot 2nd Lt. Green told men to go at approximately 800 feet. 2nd Lt. Cobb, S/Sgt. Houston and T/Sgt. Davis went out after dropping tail gunner S/Sgt. Schianca out. They didn't see chute open. Don't know about S/Sgt. Parker. 2nd Lt. Cobb says people on the ground say chute opened about 40 feet off ground. 2nd Lt. George O. Winberg, 0-703355, was in woods about four hours and 2nd Lt. Cobb, 0-699310, about one half hour. Picked up by Slovaks and taken to small village and handed over to gendarmes and then to Trencin, Slovakia. Next morning was taken to Bratislava. They were interrogated by Slovak Lieutenant first in charge at Bratislava and interpreter and a German officer in Slovak army. Asked general questions, silly ones like how many engines on B-24. Why bombed Bratislava. Not pressed for answers. German however wanted all bombing informations, etc. German then tried to get American airmen transferred to Vienna, Austria but Slovaks wouldn't allow that.

Waist Gunner S/Sgt. Jesse C. Houston, 13064943, took over both waist guns when T/Sgt. Claude H. Davis Jr., 34708368, was aiding tail gunner S/Sgt. John J. Schianca, 31106819. When S/Sgt. Houston got order to leave, he went to escape hatch and opened same. 2nd Lt. Cobb threw out tail gunner, S/Sgt. Houston followed at 6-700 feet. Chute opened at 100 feet off ground. He saw crashed ship and identified bodies of Pilot 2nd Lt. Green, Copilot 2nd Lt. Gulledge, radio operator T/Sgt. Elliott and ball gunner S/Sgt. Parker.

Landed among civilians, ran for hills. Tried to evade pursuit. Got located as to area. Tried to identify people. Saw nothing, rested for two hours. Got lined up with valley which he had to cross along with a river. Started to cross road and was picked up by Slovaks. Everyone stayed away but one, he said to come with him. S/Sgt. Houston went with him. Went to village through back door of house. Thought that man was OK. Ate and then came gendarmes, reached for gun, but was stopped. Then went by aircraft to Trencin, Slovakia under guidance of gendarmes who were friendly.

S/Sgt. John James Schianca, 31106819, 464th BG, 778th BS, born 3 Jan 1915, enlisted 23 Apr 1942, MIA 7 Jul 1944, interrogated 18 Sep 1944, duty as tail gunner.

Target Blechhammer, Poland: aircraft hit by flak over target, two engines went out, losing gas, hydraulic system out, controls out. Ship struggled to Czechoslovakia. Six men bailed out: 2nd Lt. George O. Winberg, 0-703355; 2nd Lt. Neal T. Cobb, 0-699310; T/Sgt. Claude H. Davis Jr., 34708368; S/Sgt. Gerald E. Howland, 37109806; S/Sgt. Jesse C. Houston, 13064943; S/Sgt. John J. Schianca, 31106819. Four men were killed: 2nd Lt. Earcel R. Green, 0-813690; 2nd Lt. Roy L. Gulledge, 0-818145; T/Sgt. Jack E. Elliott, 13119201; S/Sgt. Andrew C. Parker, 34776541.

The aircraft B-24H Ser. No. 42-52489 crashed and burned at Belusa, Slovakia. S/Sgt. John J. Schianca landed in woods with leg injured by flak. Slovak farmers made a seat from the chute harness and carried him into the town of Trencin supervised by gendarmes who came to the crash. S/Sgt. John J. Schianca remained in hospital at Trencin where he was operated on and flak removed until 23 Aug 1944 when he was taken to prison camp. On 2 Sep 1944 the Germans came to Bratislava, Slovakia and prison guards at Grinava Prison Camp deserted and the prisoners escaped. American prisoners broke up into small groups. Five men headed northeast to the mountains. At 1400 they reached Modre. There a farmer called to them, took them in, fed them and gave them civilian clothes, maps and compasses. On 3 Sep 1944 at 0730 hours upon advice of the farmer, name unknown, they headed toward Banska Bystrica. In the mountains they met Slovak soldiers who were escaping. One agreed to accompany them and get them through. On 3 Sep 1944 they arrived at Casta at 1400 hours where they stayed with civilians.

On 4 September at 0930 hours they left Casta and went thru Dolni Oresany, skirted Horni Oresany and arrived at Dolna Krupa at 1930 hours. They were fed and furnished lodging by a widow who thought they were Slovakians.

On 5 Sep 1944 at 0700 hours they left and went thru the mountains to a village where they were fed and taken by horse and carriage 15 km northeast to the woods. They crossed the Vah River by ferry then went thru the woods to Hoste. Here they stopped at a pub where they met a gendarme who got them food and lodging.

From here they all travelled Eastward to the evacuation point at Banska. Bystrica, S/Sgt. John J. Schianca returned to Italy on 17 Sep 1944.

2nd Lt. Earcel R. Green, 0-813690, private cemetery, Campbell, MO.
2nd Lt. Roy L. Gulledge, 0-818145, Chattanooga National Cemetery, Chattanooga, TN.
T/Sgt. Jack E. Elliott, 13119201, private cemetery, Richmond, VA.
S/Sgt. Andrew C. Parker, 34776541, private cemetery, Wilkesboro, NC.

7 JUL 1944, 15TH AF, 325TH FG, 316TH FS

Target: Blechhammer, Poland
Aircraft type, model and series: P51B 15NA, Serial No. 43-24895
Engine - type, model and series: V-1650-7, Serial number: V-321382
Nickname of aircraft: unknown
Type of mission: Escort
Aircraft last known position: 49/12 N, 18/25 E
Aircraft P-51B was lost as a result of explosion in mid-air at 10,000 feet
Place of Departure: Lesina, Italy

CREW POSITION, NAME IN FULL

Soltesz, Frank C.   2nd Lt, Pilot   0-697232   Lakewood, OH   POW/Evaded

ESCAPE STATEMENT

2nd Lt. Frank C. Soltesz, 0-697232, 325th FG, 318th FS, born 17 Jul 1921, enlisted 24 Jul 1942, MIA 7 Jul 1944, interrogated 8 Oct 1944, duty as fighter pilot.

2nd Lt. John E. Floyd Jr., 0-815299, Lorraine American Military Cemetery, St. Avold, France

On 7 Jul 1944, 2nd Lt. Soltesz was flying escort to a bombing mission to the Oil Refineries at Blechhammer, Poland. His aircraft was a P-51.

Over Bratislava, Czechoslovakia area, 2nd Lt. Soltesz was attacking some ME-109s when he was hit from behind by a German fighter and his aircraft went into a dive. He stayed in the ship to about 5,000 feet when the left wing fell off, then he bailed out injuring his left shoulder doing so.

2nd Lt. Soltesz landed in a village of Luka u Mujavy, Slovakia and was taken by civilians to Myjava where he received medical attention, his face being swollen and bleeding due to the canopy of the cockpit having been shot off.

Here he was given a good meal and drinks from the Slovaks and handed over to the police. 2nd Lt. Soltesz, who speaks Slovak, was well treated by the police.

German soldiers arrived with written orders to take him prisoner. The Slovaks refused to hand him over and took him out of the Police Headquarters, by a side door and in a car to Bratislava. Here they visited the Ministry, but as all officials had left, 2nd Lt. Soltesz was taken to the hospital.

On 8 Jul 1944, 2nd Lt. Soltesz was taken to the Ministry and saw Slovak General Chotlos, who tried unsuccessfully to interrogate him.

He then returned to the hospital for a few hours and was moved to the "The Academy" Main Camp at Bratislava with other American prisoners. At this camp, 2nd Lt. Soltesz was put into one room with another American officer and the door locked on them until 2nd Lt. Soltesz complained in Slovak to the 2nd Lt. guard; after this occasion they were allowed to visit other officers after interrogation. Food was brought up to the prisoners in their rooms for the first two weeks. After this they ate in the mess hall. A Slovak captain occasionally visited the prisoners and ate with them.

Civilians called at the camp from time to time and left food for the prisoners. They also brought cigarettes. One Slovak soldier used to bring the prisoners 1-1/2 to 2 lbs. of butter each week.

On 12 Aug 1944 the whole camp was moved to Grinava Camp. The journey being made in a bus with guards, followed by a car with Slovak officers. Treatment at this camp was good and prisoners were given more liberties. A volley ball court was "in limits" and swimming facilities allowed to prisoners under guards. The commanding officer allowed prisoners to listen to the radio.

On 1 Sep 1944, a Slovak soldier told 2nd Lt. Saltesz that Germans were in Bratislava. The CO of the camp verified this by visiting the town. On night 1-2 Sep 1944 the CO left with the Slovak soldiers to find transport to evacuate the prisoners.

Front Row, kneeling l-r: S/Sgt. Leo S. Kituskie, Sgt. Ernest H. Coleman, Sgt. Rodger I. Diamond, Sgt. Raymond H. Brown. Back Row, standing l-r: 2nd Lt. Earl R. Dubas, F/O Howard D. Mooers, 2nd Lt. Leroy "Buzzy" A. Radovich, S/Sgt. Thomas O. Moloney. Sgt. William F. Helmcke and F/O Irving Groskind are not in picture.

As he did not return within the specified time the prisoners went off in small groups to make their way among the hills to Banska Bystrica where they heard they could obtain escape help. 2nd Lt. Frank C. Soltesz traveled with 2nd Lt. George O. Winberg, 0-703355, and 2nd Lt. Neal T. Cobb, 0-699510, in the hills to Dobra Voda having obtained civilian clothes on the way, thence with a civilian guide to Brasova, where they contacted Slovak Partisans, who promised to help them to escape to Banska Bystrica where they could be evacuated by the Slovak Army.

After four days with the Partisans, Americans were given heavier civilian clothing and contacted another 12 Americans from this camp. They then left on 9 Sep 1944 having been given a route by the Partisans and obtaining food from civilians, reached Lehota on 14 Sep 1944. Here they picked up a guide and left on 15 Sep 1944 for Cimena where they changed guides and reached Podlusany. On 17 Sep 1944 contacted some Partisans and moved with another guide the following morning for Zvolen where was another Partisan group. After that American group reached Banska Bystrica where they contacted the American Mission. On 7 Oct 1944 they were evacuated from Tri Duby A/D to Italy.

7 JUL 1944, 15TH AF, 52ND FG, 5TH FS

Target: Blechhammer, Poland
Aircraft type model and series: P51C NA, Serial No. 42-103503
Engine - Type, model and series: V-1650-7, Serial number: 7-320487
Nickname of aircraft: unknown, SQN Letters, VF-Y

Sgt. Raymond H. Brown

Type of mission: Bomber escort

Aircraft last sighted at 1035 hours in a 60' dive to the deck.
Aircraft was lost as a result of unknown circumstances
Place of departure: Madna, Italy

CREW POSITION, NAME IN FULL

Floyd, John E. Jr.	2nd Lt, Pilot	0-815299	Tuscaloosa, AL	KIA

7 JUL 1944, 15TH AF, 454TH BG, 737TH BS

Target: Odertal, Germany
Aircraft type, model and series: B-24-H, Serial No. 42-95380
Engines - type, model and series: R-1830-43
Engine Nos. (a) CP-306151 (b) CP-309588 (c) CP-306318 (d) CP-306281
Nickname of aircraft: *Buffalo Gal*
Type of mission: Bombing
Aircraft was lost as a result of enemy aircraft. Aircraft last seen at approximately 1240 hours 47/10 N, 17/30 E.
Point of departure: San Giovanni, Italy

CREW POSITION, NAME IN FULL

Dubas, Earl R.	2nd Lt, Pilot	0-817181	Pittsburgh, PA	POW
Radovich, Leroy A.	2nd Lt, Copilot	0-763725	Oakland, CA	POW
Mooers, Howard D.	F/O, Nav.	T 125597	Cape May, NJ	POW
Groskind, Irving	F/O, Bomb.	T 123319	Memphis, TN	POW

B-24H Ser. No. 42-64481, "Ohmyachinback," 7 Jul 1944 over occupied Czechoslovakia. five minutes before crew members bailed out.

2nd Lt. David H.R. Loughrie, 0-821306, 7 Jun 1944, New Mexico

Moloney, Thomas O.	S/Sgt, Eng.	33237275	Saratoga, NY	POW
Kituskie, Leo S.	S/Sgt, RO	33621168	Gilbertan, PA	POW
Diamond, Rodger I.	Sgt, AG	33243758	York, PA	POW
Brown, Raymond H.	Sgt, AG	15340236	Thornton, IL	POW
Helmcke, William F.	Sgt, AG	36724542	Calumet City, IL	POW
Coleman, Ernest H.	Sgt, AG	33645839	Vilson, VA	Evadee/POW
Bulfin, Frank J.	Cpl, AG	37413112	St. Louis, MO	Evadee/POW

STATEMENT BY 2ND LT. EARL RAYMOND DUBAS, 0-817181

On our 14th mission to Odertal, Germany we were forced to bail out. F/O Mooers, Sgt. Diamond, Sgt. Brown, Sgt. Helmcke, F/O Groskind all bailed out at 1245 near Lake Balaton, Hungary. Cpl. Bulfin, S/Sgt. Kituskie, S/Sgt. Moloney and Sgt. Coleman bailed out over Czechoslovakia and were helped by partisans.

STATEMENT BY S/SGT. LEO S. KITUSKIE, 33621168

I bailed out near Trencin, Slovakia on 7 Jul 1944 at about 1200 hours at an altitude of 1700 feet, after ship had been hit by enemy fighters.

I saw two men jump and saw their two chutes in the air. They were Cpl. Bulfin and S/Sgt. Moloney. I was in the hospital later with Cpl. Bulfin and S/Sgt. Moloney in Trencin and last I saw Cpl. Bulfin an 2 Sep 1944 at P/W camp in Pezinok, Slovakia. On that day all left camp and I became separated from Cpl. Bulfin.

7 JUL 1944, 15TH AF, 455TH BG, 741ST BS

Target: Odertal, Germany
Aircraft type, model and series: B-24-H, Serial No. 42-64481

Engines - type, model and series: R-1830-65
Engine Nos. (a) DP-42-91539 (b) DP-42-5927 (c) DP-42-91029 (d) DP-42-91203
Nickname of aircraft, *Ohmyachinback*
Type of mission: bombing
Aircraft last sighted at 1149 hours, 49/20 N, 18/25 E. Aircraft was lost as a result of enemy antiaircraft fire.
Point of departure: San Giovanni, Italy

CREW POSITION, NAME IN FULL

Chadwick, Ralph M.	1st Lt Pilot	0-690048	Oklahoma City, OK	POW
Loughrie, David H.R.	2nd Lt, Copilot	0-821306	Baltimore, MD	POW
Grimm, John N.	1st Lt, Bomb.	0-695491	Buffalo, NY	POW
Daly, Philip J.	T/Sgt, RO	39325328	Lakeview, OR	POW
Schindler, Sol D.	S/Sgt, RO	32020283	West New York, NY	POW
Steinhauer, Norman M.	T/Sgt, Eng.	16134001	Milwaukee, WI	POW
Anderson, Horace R.	S/Sgt, Eng.	37341462	Fort Collins, CO	POW
Delaney, William A.	S/Sgt, Gunner	39203617	Port Townsend, WA	POW
Earl, Adrian	S/Sgt, Gunner	36258274	Macon, GA	POW

7 JUL 1944, ODERTAL, GERMANY

REPORT

On 7 Jul 1944 toward 12:00 o'clock an enemy aircraft, a four motored Liberator bomber type B-24, was shot-down in flames and crashed in the vicinity of Blauendorf, District of Novy Jicin. In the enclosed report five crew members who parachuted, four of these were captured by Air Command "Miethe" near Frydek, further more one could have been captured by the Gendarmerie in Seitendorf.

The following are the persons captured:
1) Schindler, Sol David, born 24 Dec 1920, Brooklyn
2) Earl, Adrian, born 28 Aug 1921, Chicago
3) Anderson, Horace Richard, born 24 Apr 1923, Fort Collins
4) Delaney, William, 19 years old, personalities refused to be given by prisoner.
5) Steinhauer, Max, born 29 Jul 1922, Milwaukee, WI.

Concerning the whereabouts of the above crew members, up to now nothing is known. One man burned in the machine (?). The captured will be transferred to the Army Garrison Commander in Moravska Ostrava. The salvage of machine will be taken over by the Air Base at Prossnitz.

7 JUL 1944, 15TH AF, 454TH BG, 736TH BS

Target: Odertal Oil Refinery, Germany
Aircraft type, model and series: B-24H, Serial No. 42-52173
Engines - type, model and series: R-1830-43
Engine Nos. (a) CP-300744 (b) BP-428890 (c) BP-446881 (d) BP-428558
Nickname of aircraft: Unknown
Type of mission: Bombing
Aircraft was lost as a result of anti-aircraft fire. Aircraft B-24H was not seen and no other information is available.
Point of departure: San Giovanni, Italy

CREW POSITION, NAME IN FULL

| Wilson, John B. | 1st Lt, Pilot | 0-669824 | Fitchburg, MA | POW/Evadee |
| Terry, Maurice W. | 2nd Lt, Copilot | 0-1691683 | Brazil, IN | POW/Evadee |

2nd Lt. Leon H. Polinsky
21 Jul 1944, Brux, Czechoslovakia

Rothermal, Gerald K.	2nd Lt, Nav.	0-688469	Reading, PA	POW/Evadee
Fernandes, George L.	2nd Lt Bomb.	0-688745	Norfolk, VA	POW
Rienerth, Karl G.	T/Sgt, Eng.	35587495	Youngstown, OH	POW/Evadee
Hede, Robert E.	T/Sgt, RO	16142944	Cicero, IN	POW
Yezdich, Nick	T/Sgt, WG	35273356	Akron, OH	POW/Evadee
Fleharty, Robert J.	S/Sgt, NG	35666707	Cincinnati, OH	POW/Evadee
La Fond, Archie M.	S/Sgt, TG	19003242	Visalia, CA	KIA
Benner, Charles V. Jr.	S/Sgt, BG	12054392	Trenton, NJ	POW/Evadee

ESCAPE STATEMENT

2nd Lt. Maurice W. Terry, 0-1691683, 454th BG, 736th BS, born 5 Jun 1919, enlisted 12 Oct 1940, MIA 7 Jul 1944, interrogated 8 Oct 1944, duty as copilot.

2nd Lt. Gerald K. Rothermal, 0-688469, 454th BG, 736th BS, born 9 Apr 1920, enlisted 15 Oct 1941, MIA 7 Jul 1944, interrogated 18 Sep 1944, duty as navigator.

T/Sgt. Karl G. Rienharth, 35587495, 454th BG, 736th BS, born 8 Dec 1909, enlisted 5 Aug 1922, MIA 7 Jul 1944, interrogated 8 Oct 1944, duty as engineer-gunner.

T/Sgt. Nick Yezdich, 35273356, 454th BG, 736th BS, born 27 Nov 1918, enlisted 2 Feb 1942, MIA 7 Jul 1944, interrogated 8 Oct 1944, duty as waist gunner

7 JUL 1944, ODERTAL OIL REFINERY, GERMANY

Three ME-109s followed line of chutes, evidently counting men who had bailed out. Radioman T/Sgt. Robert E. Hede, 16142944, badly injured in arm and shoulder, but was able to go out thru waist window. One burst of flak slightly injured pilot 1st Lt. John B.

The original crew of 2nd Lt. Leon H. Polinsky. Standing in front of B-24 "Texan Hellcat" (the aircraft was shot-down on 26 Jun 1944). L-R: 2nd Lt. Leon H. Polinsky, F/O Eben H. Tilman, 2nd Lt. John Tropea (not on mission), 2nd Lt. Charles Denbo. Kneeling L-R: T/Sgt. Tunis Gaalswyk, T/Sgt. Marlin S. Kerby, T/Sgt. Kenneth Mc Laughlin (not on mission), T/Sgt. Robert O. Finley, S/Sgt. Colby A. Davis, T/Sgt. John Warnock (MIA on 7 May 1944 with another crew). Aircraft B-24G, Serial No. 42-78432 "Final Approach."

Wilson, 0-669824, and Copilot 2nd Lt. Maurice W. Terry, 0-1691683, about two minutes before bombs away. Our ship was seen to crash into mountains.

2nd Lt. Maurice W. Terry, 0-1691683, landed and was soon picked up by Slovak gendarmes. He was taken to Trencin with S/Sgt. Charles W. Benner, 12054392. Gendarmes took T/Sgt. Nick Yezdich, 35273356, and T/Sgt. Robert E. Hede, 16142944, to hospital in Trencin, Slovakia. T/Sgt. Karl G. Rienerth spent two days in woods when Slovak soldiers picked him up and took him to Trencin.

T/Sgt. Nick Yezdich stayed in hospital two weeks, then he was flown by Slovak Captain to Bratislava. Other three were taken to Bratislava after one night in Trencin. All stayed in Bratislava Prison Camp, soldiers barracks and a cavalry school until 12 Aug 1944. On 16 Aug 1944 they arrived at Grinava, 14 kilometers north of Bratislava. Prisoners departed Grinava on 2 Sep 1944 at 0200 hours.

Group included 31 American prisoners and Slovak soldiers. The men were promised trucks in case the Germans were coming. They were told if trucks did not arrive to take off on their own which they did at 0200 hours.

After leaving camp these men took to the hills and then spent 19 days walking until they reached Banska Bystrica on 21 Sep 1944, the place of evacuation.

S/Sgt. Archie M. La Fond, 19203242, private cemetery, California.

21 JUL 1944, 15TH AF, 454TH BG, 736TH BS

Target: Brux, Czechoslovakia
Aircraft type, model and series: B-24G, Serial No. 42-78432
Engines - type, model and series: R-1830-65A
Engine Nos.: (a) BP-438756 (b) BP-438999 (c) BP-438925 (d) BP-438026
Nickname of aircraft: Unknown
Type of mission: Bombing
Aircraft was lost as a result of enemy anti-aircraft fire. Last seen at 1210 hours approximately 50/34 N, 13/42 E.
Point of departure: San Giovanni, Italy

Leon H. Polinsky, 6 Jun 1942, Bakersfield, CA

2nd Lt. Leon H. Polinsky 0-1691862, Lorraine American Military Cemetery, St. Avold (Moselle), France

Crew position, name in full

Polinsky, Leon H.	2nd Lt, Pilot	0-1691862	Smithfield, TX	KIA
Tilman, Eben H.	F/O, Copilot	T-123190	Boise, ID	POW
Denbo, Charles	2nd Lt, Nav.	0-1691697	Pulaski, TN	POW
Gaalswyk, Tunis	T/Sgt, Eng.	39550620	Artesia, CA	KIA
Finley, Robert O.	T/Sgt, RO	36433534	Chester, IL	KIA
Maulding, Lee R.	T/Sgt, BTG	20819698	Austin, TX	POW
Kerby, Marlin S.	T/Sgt, TTG	37231728	Bonner Springs, KS	POW
Long, Richard W.	S/Sgt, WG	31204896	Greenwood, MA	POW
Davis, Colby A.	S/Sgt, WG	11122580	Hebron, ME	POW
Middleton, Alton L.	S/Sgt, NTG	18214085	Mart, TX	POW

Flight Officer Leon H. Polinsky, a 1938 graduate of North Side High, enlisted in the Air Force in September 1940. On 7 Dec 1941 he was en route to the Philippine Islands as a ground crew member. The ship, 450 miles out from the Pacific Coast, returned and Leon was accepted for air cadet training. He won his wings and was appointed a flight officer on 20 May 1943 at Stockton Field, CA.

21 JUL 1944, 15TH AF, 456TH BG, 744TH BS

Target: BRUX (Most) Synthetic Oil Plant Buildings, Czechoslovakia
Aircraft type, model and series: B-24H, Serial No. 42-64501
Engines - type, model and series: R-1830-65
Engine Nos. (a) BP-428696 (b) CP-305657 (c) BP-428617 (d) 42-40315
Nickname of aircraft: Unknown
Type of mission: Bombing

Aircraft was lost as a result of being struck by another aircraft. Aircraft B-24H seen to explode in mid-air at 1208 over target area.

Point of Departure: Stornara Field, Italy

CREW POSITION, NAME IN FULL

Eide, Gunnar	2nd Lt, Pilot	0-696445	Minneapolis, MN	KIA
Dingwall, James N.	F/O, Copilot	T-61738	New York, NY	POW
Theim, John V.	2nd Lt, Nav.	0-712699	Mountain Lakes, NJ	KIA
Powell, George S.	S/Sgt, RWG	38385524	Lake Providence, LA	KIA
Powell, Leo A.	S/Sgt, LWG	39695993	Sanger, CA	POW
Elder, Arthurn	Pvt, NG	11071738	Oklahoma City, OK	KIA
Wesson, James L.	Sgt, TTG	34801459	Tuscaloosa, AL	KIA
Hansen, Clayton W.	Sgt, BG	12133627	Perth Amboy, NJ	KIA
Hall, Francis T.	Sgt, TG	31306012	Quincy, MA	KIA

STATEMENT BY 2ND LT WARREN E. ASKEW

I was flying as a copilot on aircraft #878 on 21 July 1944, in position Charley 6. Just after the bombs had been dropped on the target and after the formation had cleared the flak area, I saw 2nd Lt G. Eide's aircraft # 42-64501 flying Charley 2 position disintegrate in mid-air for no apparent reason. The time of the explosion was approximately 1209, and at about 50-36N, 13-57E. No parachutes were seen to open.

STATEMENT BY CAPTAIN MARVIN E. WHITE

Interrogation of combat crew members flying in Charley Box on 21 July 1944 state that aircraft #42-64501, flown by 2nd Lt. Gunnar Eide, was last seen at approximately 1209 hours when it collided with another aircraft (#42-78306).

STATEMENT BY S/SGT LEO A. POWELL 39695993 (RADIO OPERATOR, AWG)

About one minute after hitting target, another ship (#42-78306), disabled by flak and out of control, ran into right wing of our ship and tore it off. Ship tossed around. I tried to get out and couldn't, but was evidently thrown thru the hatch. I saw four chutes, one empty and three with men, in addition to my own.

I landed safely and was immediately captured. Met the other three men after capture. Copilot (F/O James N. Dingwall T-61738), whose name I do not recall, was the only man out of my ship. The other two were officers from ship that crashed into us (1st Lt. Sidney H. Brooks 0-808945, and 2nd Lt. James J. Duston 0-671232), whose names I do not recall. Can only conclude that remainder of crews of both ships (seven men in mine) died in crash.

We four (S/Sgt. G.S. Powell, F/O J.N. Dingwall, 1st Lt. S.H. Brooks, 2nd Lt. J.J. Duston) were taken to town near Brux (Most) after capture, and from there to POW camp near Frankfurt-on-Main.

I lost sight of the Copilot F/O J.N. Dingwall, the only other survivor from my ship, when he went from Dulag Luft to Officers' Prison camps with the two oficers surviving from the other ship. This man was not a regular member of our crew, I went to an enlisted man's camp, and eventually was repatriated by Allied advance.

GERMAN AIR FLEET COMMAND, TACTICAL GROUP, GENERAL STAFF SECTION

AIR ATTACK ON BRUX (MOST) ON 21 JUL 1944

Crash of two bombers in city area of Teplitz (Teplice). The few personal effects and flight property will be well guarded, which were found by the recovered dead of the two crashed American bombers, as well as the delivery of map and book instruction material will be transmitted upon further orders. The eight burned fliers bags were by a master sergeant of the Anti-Aircraft group at Brux, in the presence of the Staff Officer, Sgt. Nickel, opened and each contained 48 dollars in ten, five and one dollar notes, five single dollar notes were found loose.

Several burned fliers lay under the wreckage of the aircraft, and in the wreckage there are large quantities of ammunition of which the Salvage Command Fliers Station, Area Prag (PRAHA) were as yet unable to recover.

It is very clear that of the 14 dead, only eight fliers bags or wallets are guarded for safe-keeping. Furthermore only a part of the I.D. tags of the crashed burned fliers are guarded for safe keeping. Many of the tags as well as personal belongings lay scattered in the country and it can not be established to which individual they belonged as well as the ring and watch which were found. Most probably that the salvage of the unburned wreckage by the Salvage Command, Prag (Praha) that more fliers wallets and personal effects will be found.

MEMBERS OF CREWS FROM AMERICAN AIRPLANES THAT CRASHED DOWN ON 21 JUL 1944 ABOUT 1225 AT TEPLICE.

Name	Number
Arthur Elder	11071738
John V. Theim	0-712699
Roy S. Dubs	0-692770
Clayton W. Hansen	12133627
Francis T. Hall	31306012
Carl Ezuck	37301152
Gunnar Eide	0-696445
James L. Wesson	34801459
Edward W. Broom	18150346
Robert M. Gafner	39557533
Andrew R. Smyth	35621118

The indentification tags of 11 men were found in the wreckage of the plane, Presumably most of the indentification tags were not carried properly. Therefore the indentity could not be established in some cases and the physician had to write "unknown" on the respective certificates of death.

Furthermore two rings were taken away from the bodies:
1) One wedding ring (gold 14 carat) engraving GSP 10-.31-.38 (G.S.Powell)
2) One friendship ring (platinum 10 carat) no engraving
3) One coin (half a dollar) and Talisman with two ID-tags of Sgt. Clayton W. Hansen

GERMAN ARMED FORCES, 3RD INF. BTL. 942, TEPLITZ (TEPLICE)

Certificate of places of graves, for 14 members of American crews. Teplice Cemetery 24 Section 10th Row (for all 14)

Grave No. 3	Arthur Elder
Grave No. 4	John V. Theim
Grave No. 5	Roy S. Dubs
Grave No. 6	Clayton W. Hansen
Grave No. 7	Francis T. Hall
Grave No. 8	Carl Ezuck
Grave No. 9	Gunnar Eide
Grave No. 10	James L. Wesson
Grave No. 11	Edward W. Broom
Grave No. 12	Robert M. Gafner
Grave No. 13	Andrew R. Smyth
Grave No. 14*	Unknown American Airman
Grave No. 15*	Unknown American Airman
Grave No. 16*	Unknown American Airman

*Grave No's 14, 15, 16 in unknown order: Arthur P. Arseneaux 306, George B. Youngquist 306, George S. Powell 501

S/Sgt. George S. Powell, 38385524, Lorraine American Military Cemetery, St. Avold (Moselle), France

2nd Lt. John V. Theim, 0-712699, the Ardennes American Military Cemetery, Neuville-en-Condroz, Belgium

26 JUL 1944, TEPLITZ/TEPLICE, CZECHOSLOVAKIA

CERTIFICATES OF DEATH

ARMY PHYSICIAN, TEPLICE-SANOV, 24 JUL 1944

Unknown dead in USA uniform and pilot's combination suit. Stature approximately 5 Ft. 9 in. (172 cm). Cause of death: Brain smashed, complicated fractures of upper and forearms, interior injuries caused by crash of plane on 21 Jul 1944.

Unknown dead dressed in USA uniform and pilot's combination suit. Stature approximately 6 Ft. 3in. (187 cm). Cause of death: Fracture of skull with smashed head caused by crash of plane.

Unknown dead dressed in USA uniform and pilot's combination suit. Stature approximately 6 Ft. (180 cm), Cause of death: Fracture of skull, interior injuries, complicated fracture of leg, caused by crash of aircraft on 21 Jul 1944.

Unknown dead dressed in USA uniform and pilot's combination suit. Stature approximately 6 Ft. 2 in. (185). Cause of death: Fracture of skull, interior injuries, caused by plane crash.

Unknown dead dressed in USA uniform and pilot's combination suit. Stature approximately 5 Ft. 11 in. (178 cm). Cause of death: Head smashed, interior injuries, caused by crash of airplane

Unknown dead, dressed in USA uniform and pilot's combination suit. Stature approximately 6 Ft. (181 cm), Cause of death: Smashed skull, interior injuries, caused by crash of aircraft on 21 Jul 1944.

Unknown dead, dressed in USA uniform and pilot's combination suit. Stature approximately 6 Ft. 1 in. (183 cm). Cause of death: Skull smashed, complicated fractures, thigh, leg, and arm fractures, caused by crash of aircraft on 21 Jul 1944

Unknown dead, dressed in USA uniform and pilot's combination suit. Stature approximately 5 Ft. 10 in. (176 cm). Cause of death: Skull smashed, complicated arm and leg fractures, caused by crash of aircraft on 21 Jul 1944.

Crew of 1st Lt. Sidney H. Brooks and 2nd Lt. Roy S. Dubs. Standing in unknown order: 1st Lt. Sidney H. Brooks, 2nd Lt. Roy S. Dubs, 2nd Lt. James J. Duston and unknown. Sitting and kneeling, on left: S/Sgt. Robert M. Gafner and in unknown order S/Sgt. George B. Youngquist, S/Sgt. Carl Ezuck, S/Sgt. Arthur P. Arseneaux, S/Sgt. Andrew R. Smith, T/Sgt. Edward W. Broom.

Unknown dead in completely charred condition. Burned by crash of plane on 21 Jul 1944.
Unknown dead in a completely charred condition. Burned by crash of aircraft on 21 July
Unknown dead in completely charred condition. Cause of death: Burned by crash of aircraft.
Unknown dead in completely charred condition. Cause of death: Burned in crashed aircraft on 21 Jul 1944.
Unknown dead in completely charred condition. Cause of death: Burned in crashed aircraft on 21 Jul 1944.
Unknown dead in completely charred condition. Cause of death: Burned in aircraft crash on 21 Jul 1944.
All above bodies of American airmen have no Identity-Tags or identification papers.

Surgeon-major and local Army Physician
(name illegible)

21 Jul 1944, 15th AF, 456th BG, 746th BS

Target: Brux (Most) Synthetic Oil Plant Buildings, Czechoslovakia
Aircraft type, model and series: B-24G, Serial No. 42-78306
Engines - type, model and series: R-1830-65

S/Sgt. Robert M. Gafner and his wife Crystal

S/Sgt. Robert M. Gafner

Engine Nos. (a) BP-432454 (b) BP-432345 (c) BP-432540 (d) BP-432315
Nickname of aircraft: Unknown
Type of mission: bombing
Aircraft was lost as a result of collision with another aircraft. Aircraft B-24G last sighted at 1208 over target area.
Point of Departure: Stornara Field, Italy

CREW POSITION, NAME IN FULL

Brooks, Sidney H.	1st Lt, Pilot	0-808945	Douglas, GA	POW
Dubs, Roy S.	2nd Lt, Copilot	0-692770	Harrisburg, PA	KIA
Duston, James J.	2nd Lt, Nav.	0-671232	Roslindale, MA	POW
Gafner, Robert M.	S/Sgt, Bomb.	39557533	Warren, PA	KIA
Broom, Edward W.	T/Sgt, RWG	18150346	New Orleans	KIA
Smyth, Andrew R.	S/Sgt, NG	35621118	Columbus, OH	KIA
Arseneaux Arthur P.	S/Sgt, TTG	11117368	Cambridge, MA	KIA
Ezuck, Carl	S/Sgt, BG	37301152	Minneapolis, MN	KIA
Youngquist, George B.	S/Sgt, TG	37546096	North Branch, MN	KIA

STATEMENT BY T/SGT. FREDERICK W. KAUPP

We had completed the bomb run and were rallying. We expected to rally to the right, but Able box turned to the left to avoid flak. Baker rallied to the right. In an attempt to rejoin the group, Lt. Sidney H. Brook's aircraft was seen to collide with another in Charley box, which had swung underneath Baker box in the turn. Lt. Brook's aircraft was seen to go into a tight flat spin. Three parachutes were seen to open (1st Lt. Sidney H. Brooks, 2nd Lt. James J. Duston, "?") and the aircraft crashed to the ground and exploded.

1st Lt. Sidney Harry Brooks, 0-808945, born 21 Oct 1920, captured.
2nd Lt. James Joseph Duston, 0-671232, born 18 Mar 1919, captured.
2nd Lt. Roy S. Dubs, 0-692770, Lorraine American Military Cemetery, St. Avold, France.
S/Sgt. Robert M. Gafner, 39557533, private cemetery, California.
T/Sgt. Edward W. Broom, 18150346, not listed.
S/Sgt. Andrew R. Smyth, 35621118, private cemetery, Ohio.
S/Sgt. Arthur P. Arseneaux, 11117368, Lorraine American Military Cemetery, St. Avold, France.
S/Sgt. Carl Ezuck, 37301152, Ft. Snelling National Cemetery, Minneapolis, MN.
S/Sgt. George B. Youngquist, 37546096, private cemetery, Minnesota.

21 Jul 1944, 15th AF, 463rd BG, 772nd BS

Target: Brux (Most) Czechoslovakia
Aircraft type, model and series: B-17G, Serial No. 44-6276
Engines - type, model and series: R-1820-97
Engine Nos. (a) SW-019744 (b) SW-019872 (c) SW-019809 (d) SW-22136
Nickname of aircraft: Unknown
Type of mission: Bombing
Aircraft was not lost.
Point of departure: Celone, Italy
One crewmember bailed out deep in enemy territory.

Crew position, name in full

Carroll, David T.	F/O, Pilot	T61375
Shagets, Frank W.	2nd Lt, Copilot	0-817285

1st Lt. Sidney H. Brooks crew in unknown order. Front row, second from left is S/Sgt. Robert M. Gafner and fourth from left is S/Sgt. Carl Ezuck

Zimmerman, Virgil D.	S/Sgt, Nav.	39606392	
Orlowski, Francis P.	2nd Lt, Bomb.	0-761460	
Novak, Edward R.	T/Sgt, Eng.	20751111	
Bast, Harold I.	T/Sgt, Radio	18194435	
Thomas, Phillip	S/Sgt, LWG	39282935	
Rodrock, Victor S.	S/Sgt, RWG	17089414	
Telfer, William S.	S/Sgt, BTG,	19078501	Murdered by Gestapo.
Jahn, William F.	S/Sgt, TG	16145575	

S/SGT. WILLIAM S. TELFER, 19078501

S/Sgt. Telfer bailed out from his aircraft about 1115 hours on 21 Jul 1944. On 16 Aug 1944 German records stated:

Sgt. William Telfer was captured on 21 Jul 1944 at about 1200 at Welemin (Velemin 13 km NE of Brux) near Leitmerits (Litomerice) by the Gendanmery and given to the Gestapo at Leitmerits (Litomerice).

According to a statement, given by the Gendanmery, Sgt. Telfer bailed out from a formation. As far as it could be established, Sgt. Telfer broke his leg and received head and interior injuries from parachuting, on the consequences of which he died the same day at 1740.

S/Sgt. William S. Telfer was brutally killed by the Gestapo at Litomerice an 21 Jul between 1200 and 1740 hours. Cause of his death: skull fracture. Before he died he gave following information to the Gestapo killers.

William Shenon Telfer
Profession: Auto mechanic
Born: 22 Jun 1921, Iowa
Residence: Alhambra, CA
Marital: Divorced
Father: William Telfer
On 29 Jul 1944 S/Sgt. William S. Telfer was buried at Litomerice Cemetery in Grave No. 26, Field 10, Section I.

21 JUL 1944 - BRUX (MOST), CZECHOSLOVAKIA

STATEMENT BY 2ND LT FRANK W. SHAGETS, COPILOT ON SHIP #276

On Friday, 21 Jul 1944, while participating on a combat mission to Czechoslovakia fire broke out in the radio room. The radio operator T/Sgt Harold I. Bast reported same immediately after bombs away. After reporting the fire T/Sgt Bass proceeded to work to put the flame under control.

The ball turret gunner on this mission was S/Sgt. William S. Telfer, who upon seeing the smoke that filled the waist and tail of the ship made his bail-out exit from the waist door. The tail gunner S/Sgt. William F. Jahn, reported seeing S/Sgt. Telfer's parachute open.

S/Sgt. Telfer bailed out just at the time of our right turn off the bomb run and as we had a right drift, S/Sgt. Telfer had high possibilities of a safe landing without severe injuries.

STATEMENT BY T/SGT. EDWARD R. NOVAK

We had just completed our bombing run. The bomb bay doors were coming close. When fire broke out in the radio room. The pilot told the ball turret gunner S/Sgt. W.S. Telfer to come up. I went to the radio room with fire extinguisher. The flames were bursting and the smoke was so thick it was hard to see.

The radio man and I were putting the fire out. I did not see the ball turret gunner at any time during the fire or after, so do not know when he jumped.

Forest Lawn Memorial Park Glendale Cemetery in California, the last resting place of S/Sgt. William S. Telfer, 19078501, who was beaten to death by Gestapo on 21 Jul 1944 between 1200 and 1740 hours at Litomerice, occupied Czechoslovakia

STATEMENT BY T/SGT. HAROLD I BAST

After completing our bomb run, a piece of flak hit the right hand side of the radio room, hitting the hydrogen generator and causing it to burst into flames. The pilot called for the ball turret gunner S/Sgt. W.S. Telfer to come out as I called out " Fire."

I grabbed the fire extinguisher and pointed it towards the fire. When the ball turret gunner came up, the ship, from radio room back, was filled with smoke and flame. He saw the worst of it. That is all I could truthfully say about the ball turret gunner,

STATEMENT BY S/SGT. PHILLIP THOMAS

We were just coming of the target Brux, when we got hit in the radio room and flames broke out. When we used the fire extinguisher it filled the ship from the radio room on back with smoke. I kicked the main entrance door off to let some air in the ship.

Just at that time the pilot called the ball turret gunner S/Sgt. W.S. Telfer to come out. When he got out the place was full of smoke and there were flames in the radio room. He snapped on his chute and came over and got a walk around bottle from me. I plugged it into a filler valve for him.

He went to the door and looked out for a couple of seconds, than came back and put the walk around bottle back, went back to the door and jumped.

STATEMENT BY S/SGT. VICTOR S. RODROCK

When S/Sgt. Telfer came out of the ball turret there was so much smoke in the waist that it was hard to breath or see. Some flame was visible coming from the radio room and it was impossible to tell where the fire was from back there. The left waist gunner S/Sgt. P. Thomas pulled the release on the main escape door to clear the smoke as much as possible.

T/Sgt Robert V. Buchholz

S/Sgt. W.S. Telfer took his chute, snapped it on, hesitated a minute at the door, then replaced the walk around bottle he'd been using and bailed out. As I remember, this would have been about 1115.

21 JUL 1944, 15TH AF, 97TH BG, 414TH BS

Target: Brux (Most), Czechoslovakia
Aircraft type, model and series: B-17G, Serial No. 42-97551
Engines - type, model and series: R-1820-97
Engine Nos. (a) SW-004305 (b) SW-009325 (c) SW-013280 (d) SW-004336
Nickname of aircraft: unknown
Type of mission: Bombing
Aircraft was lost as a result of anti-aircraft fire. Aircraft B-17G last sighted at 1205 over enemy territory.
Point of departure: Amendola, Italy

CREW POSITION, NAME IN FULL

Cunningham, John J.	2nd Lt, Pilot	0-819064	Beverly, MA	KIA
Gibson, A.C.	2nd Lt, Copilot	0-713398	Stephenville, TX	POW
Milburn, Gerald W.	F/O, Nav.	T-125759	Louisville	Murdered by Germans
Gonnet, Emile W. Jr.	2nd Lt, Bomb.	0-735307	New Orleans, LA	POW
Whitt, Cecil H.	Sgt, RO	15066243	Williamson, WV	POW
Buchholz, Robert W.	T/Sgt, AG	16027760	Tomah, WI	Murdered by Germans
Milaszewski, Casimer E.	Sgt, RVG	36598802	Detroit, MI	Murdered by Germans
McGuire, Paul E.	Sgt, LWG	17156967	Farmington, MN	POW

| Thompson, Floyd L. | T/Sgt, BTG | 18129666 | Oklahoma City, OK | POW |
| Riber, William D. | Sgt, TG | 37610768 | Decatur, IL | Murdered by Germans |

T/Sgt. Robert V. Buchholz, 16027760, graduated from Tomah high school in 1940 and enlisted in the Air Corps 31 Aug 1940. He received his basic training at Chanute Field, IL and from there was transferred to Craig Field, AL as a mechanic. On 4 Dec 1942 he entered gunnery school at Wendover Field, UT. Other training was received at Biggs Field, El Paso, TX and Davis-Monthan Field.

In November 1943 he was transferred to aviation cadet training. Because of previous training as bomber crew member he was assigned to Plant Park, Tampa, FL in February 1944. In April he was assigned MacDill Field, Tampa, FL, where he received his training as tail gunner on the B-17. T/Sgt. Buchholz left the States for overseas duty in June 1944. Mrs. Buchholz was notified by telegram about 23 Jul 1944 that Robert was missing in action as of 21 July and that his plane was shot down over Czechoslovakia. A few months later Mrs. Buchholz was notified that he was "killed in action" in fact, he was murdered by Germans on the ground. His parents, Mr. and Mrs. Emil A. Buchholz, had his body returned to Tomah, WI in 1949.

22 Jul 1944, Local Police Authority, Ossegg (Osek) Czechoslovakia

Name: Robert Buchholz, male
Profession: American pilot, bailed out
Marital state: not known, refused statement
ASN.   16027760 T 41-42
Place of death: Ossegg (Osek), Neudorfer Str.
Nationality: American
Next of kin: not known

Certificate of Death

Name: Robert Buchholz, 16027760 T 41-42, age 22 years
Place of death: Ossegg, Neudorfer Str.
Cause of death: Murdered by Germans after he landed by parachute. He was shot execution style in occiput (lower back part of the head).
Date of death: 21 Jul 1944 (American POW shot dead when trying to escape)

The War Criminals From Osek

Statement by Jan Burianek, 18 Dec 1945

Mr. Burianek stated that on 21 Jul 1944 an unknown American airman bailed out from his stricken aircraft and safely landed on the ground near Osek Cemetery and was hiding behind wooden crates to be used for green peas which were harvested by near by women. Landing on the ground was witnessed by Osek's grave digger, Alzbeta Mosseova. This German woman reported immediately to the police location where this American airman was hiding.

One German policeman nicknamed "Krasny Antonin" (Pretty Anton) shot and killed this American airman. On the spot where this American airman was murdered remained a lot of blood and the grave digger Mosseova covered it up with dirt from nearby field.

Statement By Osek Grave Digger, Alzbeta Mosseova, 13 Aug 1945

This statement was taken at interment camp at Duchcov, Czechoslovakia. Approximately one year ago one American aircraft was shot-down over Ladunk. It was around 2100 hours when I was already in bed when one local man in SA uniform by name Heinrich Sperling knocked on my window. He told me to open and remarked that they have one dead American. I opened the door and saw four men carrying body of dead American. I opened the door for them into morgue and noticed that

Sgt. William D. Riber, 37610768

body was still warm. I placed wooden block under American airman's head and noticed warm blood coming from wound in back of his head.

The grave digger also stated that she recognized only three men from group who brought body of American airman. They were: SA member Heinrich Sperling, Policemen Emil Seifert, Anton Albert, all from Osek.

These men removed from the body, ring, boots and identification tags.

On direct order from Osek Mayor Robert Burger dead American was to be buried by the wall of cemetery and not inside.

STATEMENT BY MARIE KOLLEROVA, 1946

Marie Kollerava stated that she saw American airman alive. He was captured by German farmer by name Max Poltsch and taken by him to village of Ladung. There this American was picked up by two policemen and taken away. This American was covered with blood and was strongly built with curly hair.

FINAL REPORT, 18 MAR 1946

The American airman T/Sgt. Robert V. Buchholtz, 16027760, was murdered in cold blood by German policeman Anton Albert from Osek. This murderer escaped during May 1945 and was not apprehended.

It is safe to assume that this murderer is residing in West Germany as many others who murdered American airmen who bailed out from their damaged aircraft over occupied Czechoslovakia.

The remains of T/Sgt. Robert W. Buchholz were exhumed on 12 Nov 1946.

CERTIFICATE OF INTERMENT:

The American Pilot Robert W. Buchholz, ASN 16027760 T 41-42, was brought dead by the police to the Cemetery Ossegg. He was put into a coffin and buried outside the cemetery wall.

F/O Gerald W. Milburn, 0-713398

The Mayor as Police Authority:
(name illegible)
The Mayor of the town of Ossegg (Osek), District Aussig (Usti n Labem)

22 JUL 1944, CZECHOSLOVAKIA.

Information on the death and burial of a POW Sgt. William D. Riber, 37610768.
Name: William Riber
Rank: Radio Operator Sgt
Place of birth: Decatur, IL
Date of birth: 31 Mar 1921
Date of death: 18 Aug 1944 as POW
Nationality: American
Cause of death: Injury
Kind of injury: Fracture of pelvis and rupture of bladder
Place of death: Teplice district hospital
Place of burial: Teplitz (Teplice)
Cemetery: Village cemetery
Grave number: 24 Section, 10 Row, Grave No. 17
Buried: 22 Aug 1944 at 0730 hours
The Ardennes American Military Cemetery, Neuville-en-Condroz, Belgium
2nd Lt. John J. Cunningham, 0-819064 was also buried in this cemetery.
Sgt. Casimer E. Milaszewski, 36598802, was buried in a private cemetery in Michigan.

21 JUL 1944, 15TH AF, 2ND BG, 20TH BS

Target: Brux Synthetic Oil Plant, Czechoslovakia

Aircraft type, model and series: B-17G, Serial No. 42-31789
Engines - type, model and series: R-1820-97
Engine Nos. (a) 41-57301 (b) SW-007717 (c) SW-007680 (d) SW-007518
Nickname of aircraft: Unknown
Type of mission: Obj. Bombing
Aircraft was lost as a result of enemy aircraft. Aircraft last seen at 1046 hours at approximately 47/50 N, 13/40 E.
Point of departure: Amendola, Italy

CREW POSITION, NAME IN FULL

MacKenzie, John R.	2nd Lt, Pilot	0-808858	Buffalo, NY	KIA.
Dunkelberger, Richard E.	2nd Lt, Copilot	0-819006	Burbank, CA	KIA
Rice, Loren C.	2nd Lt, Nav.	0-717695	Spokane, WA	RTD
Hartsfield, Wylie T.	2nd Lt, Bomb.	0-683130	Baton Rouge, LA	RTD
Stephenson, Reece	S/Sgt, UTG	14098428	Atlanta, GA	RTD
Rapley, Frank A.	Sgt, LTG	14067046	Davisboro, GA	KIA
Wicklund, Donald D.	Sgt, RWG	36740109	Batavia, IL	KIA
Owen, Billy B.	Sgt, LWG	16074213	Peoria, IL	RTD
Suratt, George H.	S/Sgt, RCG	14161101	Memphis, TN	RTD
Lane, Clair H.	Sgt, TG	33570693	Three Springs, PA	KIA

REPORT ON SHOT-DOWN AMERICAN AIRCRAFT

Date of crash: 21 Jul 1944 at 1055 hours.
Place of crash: Neukirchen near Altmuenster an the east slope of Miesberg, 800 meters altitude in a clearing of a young forest.
Type of capture: Fighter aircraft
Type of aircraft: Boeing (Only an undercarriage remained)
Identification of aircraft: Not known
Condition of aircraft: Entirely destroyed by crash and by fire, 100% damage. It is only practicable to reach wreckage of the aircraft by horse and wagons. Wreckage is scattered on the Altmuenster-Neukirchen Highway, forest road 2 km from Neukirchen, then 800 meters from foot path with an altitude difference of some 150 meters on slope of mountain. One engine was found in Moosbach.

21 JUL 1944 - BRUX (MOST), CZECHOSLOVAKIA

STATEMENT BY T/SGT FLOYD L. THOMPSON 18129666

I will give as much information as I can remember when we were shot-down over Brux (Most), Czechoslovakia.

I was ball-turret gunner at the time. We were hit directly over the target by flak, a bit outside of No. 1 engine. As a result we began burning. Our aircraft was pretty well under control. I left my turret for the waist, in the meantime, we made a 360° to come again over the target. During the 360° turn four of our men bailed out: Sgt. Riber, Sgt. Whitt and Sgt. McGuire are the three I can account for. I was watching when they jumped, but the fourth I cannot be sure, but I would say it was F/O Milburn.

Sgt. Milaszewski and I moved back to the tail position since the escape hatch in that position was loose and the one in the waist was jammed.

To get out of the flak, waist gunner and I rode it out. During that time I was on the interphone. I tried talking to pilot or copilot, but no response. They were rather busy of course. I could hear them talking pretty steady.

Then T/Sgt. Buchholz left the aircraft through the bomb-bay, I believe I can be sure of that. All doors from the tail to the pilot's compartment were open. I could see almost everything going on and I was watching for what pilot might do. Then another fellow worked his way to the bomb-bay. I cannot be sure whether it was the copilot or navigator (2nd Lt. Gibson, F/O Milburn). Would say it was the copilot 2nd Lt. Gibson.

The pilot who was 2nd Lt. John J. Cunningham, stayed with the aircraft to the last. Then the pilot began working his way toward the bomb-bay with someone else just in front of him, I found out later that it was the bombardier 2nd Lt. Gonnet. While this was going on, I told Sgt. Milaszewski to jump. He jumped and I came out right after, him. just as I left, turned a few somersaults, my chute opened, just in time to see the left wing blow of the plane. It began to disintegrate.

The 2nd Lt. E.W. Gonnet and I were picked up in almost the same area and I found then that he left the aircraft just ahead of the pilot 2nd Lt. J.J. Cunningham. I am yet inclined to believe that the navigator F/O G.W. Milburn was one of the four that bailed out first.

Not any of the crew was wounded when they left the aircraft. They were not killed in the crash as those damned Jerries say, because everyone of us got out.

From there I cannot say anymore, that is, as much of it as I know, but you can probably figure out what really happened to them. Maybe this makes things only worse, but it is the only way I see it.

REPORT ON SHOT-DOWN AMERICAN AIRCRAFT

Date and time aircraft was shot-down: 21 Jul 1944 at 1055 hours.
Place of crash: At Neukirchen near Altmuenster, Austria.
Type of aircraft: Boeing

CREW

Dunkelberger, R., 0-819006, rank unknown, grave location: Moosbachgraben near Neukirchen on 24 Jul 1944.
Lane, H. Clair, 33570693, rank unknown, grave location: Hochrent near Neukirchen on 26 Jul 1944.
Unknown, body not identifiable, grave location: Moosbachgraben near Neukirchen on 24 Jul 1944. (No belongings were found.)
Unknown, body not identifiable, grave location: Moosbachgraben near Neukirchen on 24 Jul 1944. (No personal belongings were found.)
Surrat, George, 14161101, S/Sgt., captured on 21 Jul 1944 at 1200 hours at Feuerkogl/Ebensee.
Hartsfield, Wylie, 0-683130, 2nd Lt., captured on 21 Jul 1944 at 1200 hours at Feuerkogl/Ebensee.
Qwen, Billy, 16074213, Sgt., captured on 21 Jul 1944 at 1200 hours at Feuerkogl/Ebensee.

RESERVE HOSPITAL WELS

SUBJECT: AMERICAN PRISONERS IN HOSPITALS

1st Lt. Rice Loren, 0-717695, with fractures of humerus - head, left clavicula, left elbow, right radius. Time of treatment: 1-2 months, operation is necessary.
T/Sgt. Stephenson Reece, 14098428, with fractures of left upper leg, left lower arm, skull concussion, chest pains. Type of treatment: 2-3 months, operation is necessary.

Address of Hospital: Reserve Hospital Wels
Date of Arrival: 22 Jul 1944
Chief Doctor: Dr. Johann Schauerstr

STATEMENT BY SGT. BILLY B. OWEN 16074213

Our aircraft left formation over Austria. Four other men bailed out. Our ship struck the ground directly below me when I opened parachute.

2ND LT. JOHN R. MACKENZIE, 0-808858

2ND LT. RICHARD R. DUNKELBERGER, 0-819006

The Engineer S/Sgt. Stephenson said that both pilot and copilot were gone when he bailed out.

S/SGT. REECE STEPHENSON, 14098428

S/Sgt. Stephenson bailed out close where I did. Last seen one day later injured in city jail. Evidently he bailed out just before the aircraft hit.

SGT. FRANK A. RAPLEY, 14067046

Last contact probably 30 minutes before we were attacked. Last seen in the ball turret. Unknown if he bailed out.

SGT. DONALD D. WICKLUND, 36740109

Sgt. Wicklund did not bail out. He was hit in the side by 20mm bullet. I felt the ship swerve sharply, swung around and saw him dropping with blood rushing out of his side. He hit the floor and didn't move.

SGT. CLAIR H. LANE, 33570693

Last seen at take-off. Probably hit in his tail position. Unknown if he bailed out.

STATEMENT BY 2ND LT. LOREN CHARLES RICE, 0-717695

Our aircraft left formation about 20 km south of Wels, Austria. Five of the crew bailed out and five of the crew were in the aircraft when it struck the ground. Five in the aircraft were killed and I believe that the personnel at the hospital in Wels, Austria know where the bodies of those killed are buried. The hospital was named Lazzaret Krankenhouse, Lazzaret A. Wels, Austria. A Doctor by the name of Hartinger was in charge of myself and engineer while we were hospitalized there and seemed to know all that happened.

SGT. CLAIR H. LANE, 33570693

Sgt. Lane did not bail out. Last seen in tail gunner position. Killed in action.

SGT. DONALD D. WICKLUND, 36740109

Sgt. Wicklund did not bail out. Last seen in right waist gunner position. Killed in action.

SGT. FRANK A. RAPLEY, 14098428

Sgt. Rapley did not bail out. Last seen in the lower ball turret. Killed in action.
Sgt. Lane, Sgt. Wicklund and Sgt. Rapley were buried at the scene of the crash by the Germans.

2ND LT. JOHN R. MacKENZIE, 0-808858

2ND LT. RICHARD E. DUNKELBERGER, 0-819006

Last contact over interphone Just before fighter attack. Believed trapped in the falling aircraft. Believed killed in the crash and buried at the scene of crash by the Germans.